CULTURES OF THE WORLD
Eritrea

Roseline NgCheong-Lum

Marshall Cavendish
Benchmark
New York

PICTURE CREDITS

Cover: © Hemis / Alamy

alt.type / Reuters: 37, 118 • Audrius Tomonis: 138 • Camerapix Library: 7, 13, 18, 22, 23, 25, 26, 39, 41, 45, 66, 73, 74, 81, 89, 92, 104, 105, 110 • Corbis: 19, 28, 29, 30, 35, 93 • Getty Images: 53, 57, 120, 121 • Lonely Planet Images: 31, 47, 50, 94, 99, 117, 128 • North Wind Pictures Archives: 24 • Photolibrary: 1, 3, 5, 6, 8, 9, 10, 11, 12, 14, 15, 16, 17, 20, 21, 27, 36, 38, 40, 43, 44, 46, 48, 49, 52, 54, 56, 59, 60, 61, 62, 63, 64, 65, 68, 70, 71, 72, 75, 76, 77, 78, 79, 80, 82, 83, 84, 85, 86, 88, 90, 91, 95, 96, 97, 98, 103, 107, 108, 109, 111, 112, 113, 114, 115, 116, 124, 125, 126, 127, 129, 131 • The Hutchison Library: 32, 33, 106 • Trip Photographic Library: 42, 100, 102, • Wikipedia: 130

PRECEDING PAGE

Thatched huts dot the hilly, sandy landscape of Keren in Eritrea.

Publisher (U.S.): Michelle Bisson
Editors: Deborah Grahame-Smith, Peter Mavrikis, Mindy Pang
Copyreader: Sherry Chiger
Designers: Nancy Sabato, Bernard Go
Cover picture researcher: Tracey Engel
Picture researcher: Joshua Ang

Marshall Cavendish Benchmark
99 White Plains Road
Tarrytown, NY 10591
Website: www.marshallcavendish.us

© Times Media Private Limited 2001
© Marshall Cavendish International (Asia) Private Limited 2011
® "Cultures of the World" is a registered trademark of Times Publishing Limited.

Originated and designed by Times Media Private Limited
An imprint of Marshall Cavendish International (Asia) Private Limited
A member of Times Publishing Limited

Marshall Cavendish is a trademark of Times Publishing Limited.

All Internet sites were correct and accurate at the time of printing. All monetary figures in this publication are in U.S. dollars.

Library of Congress Cataloging-in-Publication Data
NgCheong-Lum, Roseline .
  Eritrea / Roseline NgCheong-Lum. — 2nd ed.
      p. cm. — (Cultures of the world)
  Includes bibliographical references and index.
  Summary: "Provides comprehensive information on the geography, history,
    wildlife, governmental structure, economy, cultural diversity, peoples,
    religion, and culture of Eritrea"—Provided by publisher.
  ISBN 978-1-60870-454-5
  1. Eritrea—Juvenile literature. I. Title.
  DT393.N47 2011
  963.5—dc22   2010035973

Printed in China
7 6 5 4 3 2 1

CONTENTS

INTRODUCTION

ALTHOUGH IT IS THE YOUNGEST STATE IN AFRICA, ERITREA IS also an ancient land where human settlement goes back thousands of years. Situated in northeastern Africa, Eritrea is a land of extreme contrasts. The fertile central plateau running down the middle of the country is flanked on both sides by desert lowlands that are plagued by frequent droughts. Eritrea has one of the lowest and hottest places on Earth—Dallol, in the Danakil Depression south of the highlands. The people of Eritrea belong to several major ethnic groups who trace their origins to before 2000 B.C. Most Eritreans live in rural areas as peasants and shepherds, scratching a meager living from the unyielding earth. After decades of oppression by Italian colonialists and then by neighboring Ethiopia, Eritreans do not take their freedom for granted. They know that they need to work hard in order to create a bright future for themselves and their children.

GEOGRAPHY

People standing on top of a cliff overlooking the southern Rift Valley of Eritrea. The Great Rift Valley, which extends from Mozambique in southern Africa all the way north into the Middle East, passes near Eritrea's eastern border.

CHAPTER 1

ERITREA LIES ON THE northeastern coast of the African continent. Lining the top edge of the Horn of Africa, the country looks like a funnel—wide in the northwest and tapering to a narrow strip in the southeast.

With an area of 46,830 square miles (121,320 square kilometers), about the size of the state of Pennsylvania, Eritrea is one of the smallest countries in Africa. Its neighbors are Sudan to the northwest, Ethiopia to the south, and Djibouti to the southeast. Its northeast border runs 715 miles (1,151 km) along the Red Sea, from which Eritrea derives its name (*Mare Erythraeum* is the Latin name for "Red Sea"). Though blessed with a long coastline and strategic location along an international trade route, Eritrea has always attracted the envy of neighboring nations, especially large and landlocked Ethiopia.

A rock pool makes an interesting geographical feature in the rugged terrain of Eritrea.

In his book *Inside Africa* (1955), John Gunther called Eritrea "a thorny, forlorn splinter of desert-cum-mountain along the Red Sea."

The hills in the Mendefera district are always covered with sunny wild-flowers and lush green grass after the end of the rainy season.

Eritrean territory includes more than 350 islands in the Red Sea, notably the Dahlak Archipelago—a cluster of 209 islands in the Red Sea that rarely rise above 50 feet (15 meters) in height. Comparatively, the country's territorial waters are almost half the size of its total land area.

THREE REGIONS

Eritrea can be divided into three main sections: the central highlands, the western lowlands, and the coastal plain. These regions differ in terms of terrain, climate, and soil.

The central plateau is a narrow strip of land that runs through the middle of the country, an extension of the Ethiopian Plateau in the south. The plateau rises to 6,500 feet (1,980 m) above sea level. At its northern end it narrows into a system of eroded hills. Rivers flow through the central highlands, carving deep gorges and small plateaus called ambas (AHM-bah).

The central plateau consists of a foundation of crystalline rock covered by sedimentary rock and basalt. The soil is fertile, and the climate is favorable, which is why agriculture and population are concentrated in this region.

Although the central highlands make up only a quarter of the country's total land area, approximately half of all Eritreans live here. This region includes the Central Province and is where the towns of Asmara (the capital of Eritrea) and Keren are located.

The broken and undulating western plain slopes gradually toward the border with Sudan. It lies at an average elevation of 1,500 feet (457 m). The land here consists of sandy soil with poor water retention properties and supports mainly savannah vegetation: scattered trees, shrubs, and grasses.

Eritrea's coastal plain stretches along the Red Sea between the borders with Djibouti and Sudan. It accounts for a third of the country's total land area and encompasses the Northern Red Sea and Southern Red Sea provinces. The coastal plain falls sharply from the central plateau and is narrower in the north—10 to 50 miles wide (16—80 km)—than in the south, where it widens to include the Danakil Plain. This barren region is part of the Danakil

Lolling hills at the Gash Sethit Province of Eritrea.

Depression, which Eritrea shares with Ethiopia. The coastal plain is part of the East African Rift System, a deep valley running from Tanzania in the south to the Red Sea, created some 25 million years ago by the collision of tectonic plates. The coastal plain suffers from poor soil quality and supports little vegetation. The main towns in this region are the port cities of Massawa and Assab.

THE DAHLAK ISLANDS

Eritrea's Red Sea region contains 354 islands and islets, of which only 10 are inhabited. Some 209 islands lying off the shore opposite Massawa make up the Dahlak Archipelago. The largest island is Dahlak Kebir, with an area of 248 square miles (643 square km). It is home to 60 percent of the archipelago's 2,500 inhabitants, mainly fishermen and cattle herders.

The Dahlak Archipelago has been designated a national park to preserve its teeming marine life, which includes dolphins, sharks, dugongs, turtles, hermit crabs, and seashells. Mangroves, shoals, coral reefs, and pumice stone formed from underwater volcanoes rank among its other interesting features.

The tranquil cove of Dissei is part of the Dahlak Archipelago of Eritrea.

The government plans to develop the Dahlak Islands into tourist resorts to attract diving and beach enthusiasts while protecting the natural marine resources, one of Eritrea's most important assets. The Red Sea's saline warm waters are a colorful haven for more than 1,000 species of fish and coral.

A mountain towers over trees and travelers along the road from Asmara to Massawa.

MOUNTAINS AND RIVERS

Eritrean terrain is mountainous with tremendous topographical variation. The highest point in the country is Amba Soira, one of several mountains in the highlands. It rises to a height of 9,885 feet (3,013 m). The lowest point, 381 feet (116 m) below sea level, is inside the Kobar Sink in the Danakil Plain.

Four major rivers and numerous streams drain the central highlands, but only a few seasonal streams flow all the way to the Red Sea. The Barka and Anseba rivers flow north to the eastern coast of Sudan but stop short of reaching the Red Sea. The Gash and Tekeze rivers form parts of Eritrea's border with Ethiopia as they flow west into Sudan. The Tekeze is a tributary of the Atbara River, which later joins the Nile. The Gash crosses the western lowlands, and its upper course, known as the Mereb, flows along the border on the plateau.

CLIMATE

The altitude differences in Eritrea produce extreme variations in climate. The central plateau experiences a moderate climate with highs of 86°F (30°C) in May and near-freezing lows in December through February. In the western lowlands the hottest months of April, May, and June reach 106°F (41°C), while the coolest month is December, when temperatures average 55°F (13°C). On the coastal plain winter temperatures range between 70°F (21°C) and 95°F (35°C), while the summer, from June to September, sees temperatures rising as high as 122°F (50°C). The Danakil Depression is the hottest place in the country.

There are two rainy seasons. The "short rains" fall in March and April; the main rains last from late June to early September. The central plateau experiences the most rain, with an annual average of 16 to 20 inches (40.6 to 50.8 centimeters). The western lowlands receive less than 16 inches (40.6 cm) a year, while the coastal plain is far drier. The inner parts of the Danakil Plain are virtually rainless.

Desert trees on the Eritrean landscape of Agordat.

FLORA AND FAUNA

Decades of armed conflict and recurrent drought have taken a heavy toll on Eritrea's natural world. The massive destruction of tropical forests, accompanied by illegal hunting, resulted in the near extinction of many plant and animal species. Upon independence the government undertook strict measures to restore the country's ecological environment. Captive breeding, land reservation, reforestation, and public awareness campaigns are still being carried out with considerable success, and the country's formerly abundant flora and fauna seem to be on the road to recovery.

Trees and other plants growing in Eritrea include baobab, pine, eucalyptus, olive, aloe, and sisal. Some, like the tamarind tree, are on the endangered list. The area around Rora Habeb, a plateau southwest of the town of Nakfa in the Northern Red Sea region, has one of the last juniper forests in the country. Vegetation here survives on nocturnal condensation rather than rainfall. Shrubs and grasses associated with the savannah green the landscape of the western lowlands. Tropical flowering plants, especially acacia, bougainvillea, and jacaranda, beautify all the major towns.

Efforts to preserve the country's animal diversity have resulted in the return of elephants, leopards, gazelles, antelopes, wild hogs and donkeys, hyenas, and ostriches. Smaller animals making a comeback include rabbits, rodents, and monkeys. There are also the fish and birds of the Red Sea islands. More than 100 bird species feed on sardines and anchovies migrating through the Red Sea. Sheep, goats, cattle, and domesticated camels are

Aloe is one of the many and diverse plant species in Eritrea.

A locust in Eritrea. In great numbers, these creatures can wipe out large areas of crops.

raised by farmers and shepherds. The camel has been adopted as the national emblem for its instrumental role in transporting supplies during the war for independence.

Locusts are one of the pests in Eritrea. They compete with humans for food as they attack a wide range of crops and trees and can eat food equal to their own body weight every day.

ASMARA

Perched a mile and a half (2.4 km) high on the central plateau, Asmara became the capital of Eritrea in 1897 when the Italian colonial authorities decided to shift their administrative center here, away from the sweltering heat of the coastal town of Massawa. With a population of about 500,000 today, Asmara is the largest city in the country.

The name *Asmara* comes from *arbate asmara*, which means "they united the four." According to legend, when fighting broke out among four small villages in the region, the village women collaborated to unite their people. Another legend says that the Queen of Sheba bore King Solomon a son in this region.

Unlike most capital cities on the African continent, Asmara is safe enough for residents and tourists to roam the streets both day and night. The city features a large central market that sells vegetables, spices, clothing, baskets, and pottery among other items. But the heart of the city is Liberation Avenue, where cafés and bars abound, as do bougainvillea and jacarandas. In the evenings residents promenade along the avenue, sip coffee in the cafés, and shop in the stores.

Much of the city was built in the 1920s and 1930s. There are some tall buildings in the city center, but most houses, such as the old Italian villas, are

An aerial view of the city of Asmara.

one or two stories high. Asmara was defended by Ethiopian troops during the war for independence and so escaped the devastation sustained by towns such as Massawa and Keren. One of the oldest and most beautiful buildings in Asmara is the former Imperial Palace, built in 1897. It is now the National Museum. Among Asmara's many important buildings and places are the High Court, the City Hall, the National Bank, the Asmara Theater, the Asmara University, the Catholic Cathedral, the Khulafa el-Rashidin Mosque, and the Enda Mariam Orthodox Church.

OTHER MAJOR TOWNS

Keren is the most important highland town after the capital Asmara. Nestled amid mountains Keren, which means "highland," sits 4,567 feet (1,391 m) up on a plateau and enjoys a temperate climate. It has a large Muslim population

Another important town is Keren, situated in the highlands of Eritrea.

Locals walking along the destroyed colonial buildings in the old town of Massawa in Eritrea.

and many mosques. The lively market here attracts traders from the region, who haggle over camels, donkeys, and sheep. Keren was severely damaged in the country's struggle for independence.

About 62 miles (100 km) east of Asmara, Massawa is the country's main port and its second-largest city. It is also the largest natural deepwater port on the Red Sea coast. Causeways link the mainland part of Massawa to two islands, Batse (also known as Massawa Island) and Taulud. The port itself is on the island of Batse. Because of Massawa's strategic coastal location, it has always been an important trading center. It too suffered heavy shelling by the Ethiopians during the war for independence, but is now back in operation. Blessed with some good beaches, Massawa is a popular weekend destination for many families.

Before the border conflict with Ethiopia in 1998, Assab used to be landlocked Ethiopia's gateway to the Red Sea. Ethiopian traders brought prosperity to the town and turned it into Eritrea's largest port. But ever since the government denied its use to Ethiopia, the town has been in decline.

Few buildings in Massawa survived the war of independence undamaged.

Sprawling across the Eritrean—Ethiopian border near Djibouti, the Danakil Plain in the Danakil Depression is one of the most inhospitable places on Earth. This dramatic landscape of deserts, rocks, salt formations, and black volcano cones is one of the lowest places on Earth not covered by water. It reaches a maximum depth of 381 feet (116 m) below sea level inside the Kobar Sink. The plain boasts the world's hottest place as well: The town of Dallol experiences an annual mean temperature of 94°F (34°C). The blistering sun and strong winds make survival here impossible for most plants and animals. However, such harsh conditions have not kept commercial enterprises from exploiting mineral deposits in the depression. As early as 1912 the Italians built a railway to the region to transport potash mined in Dallol to the coast.

The little village of Badda serves as a gateway to the Danakil Depression. The fertile land here supports the cultivation of crops. Sunday markets attract camel caravans across the moon-like Danakil Plain, although sandstorms, which strike

between 1:00 and 4:00 P.M. every day, reduce visibility to less than 33 feet (10 m). The village's main attraction, however, is the turquoise Lake Badda. It sits in an ancient volcano crater some 1,313 feet (400 m) wide and 328 feet (100 m) deep.

The Danakil Depression has attracted international interest as the site of the discovery of a one-million-year-old skull. The well-preserved fossil shows characteristics of both Homo sapiens *and* Homo erectus *(the ancestor of modern humans), providing yet another link in the evolution of the human race.*

Nakfa is special in every Eritrean's heart, for it was the first town to be recaptured by liberation fighters from the Ethiopian forces in the 1970s. The national currency was named after Nakfa in 1997 to commemorate the significance of the town in the country's history.

Eritrea's smaller towns include Mendefera in the central highlands, Agordat in the western lowlands, Tio and Ed on the coast, and Teseney close to the border with Sudan.

The war-ruined town of Nakfa.

HISTORY

The Aksumite temple ruins at the Kohaitto
archaeological site in Eritrea. Sites such as these
remind present-day generations of their ancient past.

T HE DISCOVERY OF ONE OF THE oldest human fossils ever found in Eritrea hints at the length of human existence in the country. Eritrea may well be the cradle of the human species.

The first people to settle in the area came from the region of the Nile. These Nilotes occupied the northern parts of Eritrea. Later, migrants from the ancient North African kingdom of Cush inhabited the Eritrean highlands. By 1000 B.C. or earlier, Semites crossed the Red Sea from the South Arabian kingdom of Sheba and invaded the lands of the Cushitic settlers. The Semitic occupants introduced the ancient Ge'ez script, the root of the languages used in Eritrea today. They also brought camels and sheep and developed irrigation systems and hillslope terraces, thus laying Eritrea's agricultural foundations and setting the stage for the reign of the Aksumites, the first of many "outsiders" to rule Eritrea for the next three millennia before its independence.

The Governor's Palace was constructed in 1872 and was the former winter residence of Emperor Haile Selassie.

In the 16th century Eritrea was known as *Medr Bahr* (Land of the Sea).

The stele of Ezana bears records of Aksumite wars in Eritrea. Aksumite reign saw the evolution of a distinct architectural style.

THE KINGDOM OF AKSUM

The Kingdom of Aksum rose to prominence in the fourth century A.D. and flourished until the fifth century A.D. It stretched from Nubia (now Sudan) into southern Arabia (now Yemen), and then across the Red Sea into Somalia. Its capital city was in Ethiopia, but it had important towns in Eritrea as well. Aksum controlled the land and sea routes from Africa to Europe and Asia, and monopolized trade in the region. Its principal port, Adulis, was a trading center for gold, gems, incense, and other goods.

The Aksumites are known for several achievements during their reign in Eritrea. One king, Ezana, is believed to have introduced Christianity to the region. Victory over the Jewish king of Yemen, who persecuted Christians, and the arrival of Syrian missionaries, who contributed significantly to the Church, earned Aksum great prestige and consolidated its position as a powerful defender of the Church. But Adulis was destroyed in 710 A.D., and for the next few centuries Ethiopian dynasties and Muslim sultanates battled for power in Eritrea.

THE TURKO-EGYPTIAN ERA

The Ottoman Turks entered Eritrean history in the 16th century, amid a backdrop of feuding kingdoms in the region. They occupied the Eritrean coast in 1517 and took control of Massawa. However, the Portuguese and Abyssinians combined forces to take Massawa from them in 1543. Control of the town then alternated between the Turks and these opposing forces until 1562. The Turkish leader then ruled most of Eritrea for 15 years with the Abyssinian emperor, until the latter beheaded him. What followed was another tug-of-war between the Turks and the Abyssinians. Finally, in 1589, the Turks agreed to a peace deal with the Abyssinians and remained as a power in Eritrea for another three centuries.

The Egyptians were a threat in the region in the middle of the 19th century. They invaded Sudan in 1820 and penetrated Ethiopia in 1840. In 1846 they stepped onto Eritrean shores by signing a lease for Massawa. By 1853 they had conquered the western lowlands and the area around Keren, and by 1875 they had occupied more territory on the coast. However, Egyptian power in the region faded as Egypt came under the British protectorate in the 1880s. The European chapter had begun.

A Turkish-style window on a government building in Keren is a remnant of Turkish rule in Eritrea.

ITALIAN COLONY

The Italians came to Africa after the French and the British had secured their presence in the region. They established their administration in Assab in 1882 and ousted the Egyptians from Massawa in 1885. A few years later they raised their flag in Keren and Asmara. By 1889 the Italians held most of Eritrean land, and the next year they proclaimed the territory an Italian

The Abyssinian emperor was persuaded to release his Italian prisoners. The Battle of Adua was one of the biggest battles in Africa.

colony and officially named it Eritrea. Desiring Ethiopia, they clashed with the Abyssinians at Adua in 1896. The latter became the first African power to defeat a European army. The two sides later signed a treaty recognizing Italian rule over Eritrea. In 1898 Signor Martini became Eritrea's first civilian governor, and by 1910 the colony's provincial structure was in place.

The Italians built railroads, ports, plantations, and factories, and introduced modern ways of living in their colony. Eritrea soon overtook Ethiopia in material progress. By 1929 Massawa was the biggest port on the east coast of Africa, and by 1937 Eritrea was the center of a regional transportation network employing some 100,000 people.

BRITISH PROTECTORATE

In 1935 the Italians launched their planned attack on Ethiopia from their Eritrean base. Six years later, the British returned and forced them back into Eritrea. The Italians lost several towns in a matter of months. Their surrender of Asmara on April 1, 1941, sealed their defeat in Eritrea, which now faced a new master.

The British were unprepared to run a new administration and so they made few (though substantial) changes to the current one. They retained the Italian officials, but lifted the color bar and trained Eritreans in civil service and education.

The British continued to invest only while Eritrea remained useful to their North African strategy. Toward the end of World War II, in 1944, they began removing infrastructure, equipment, and remaining supplies. Eritrea's economy collapsed in 1946, plunging the country into a state of social unrest.

During the crisis Ethiopia intended to annex Eritrea, while the British proposed to partition the country between Sudan and Ethiopia. Eritrea's future was debated internationally until 1952, when the British protectorate years ended with a United Nations (UN) resolution to grant it autonomy within a federation with Ethiopia.

FEDERATION

To find out what the Eritreans themselves wanted for their future, the United Nations sent a fact-finding mission to Eritrea. However, the Commission of Enquiry, fed misinformation by the British, reported on June 28, 1949 that the Christian majority in Eritrea was in favor of union with Ethiopia.

On December 2, 1950, the United Nations passed a resolution to federate Eritrea with Ethiopia. Eritrea would be an autonomous unit governing itself under the sovereignty of Ethiopia. The federal plan took effect on September 11, 1952.

The British war cemetery on the edge of the town of Keren testifies to a major battle in 1941, in which the British defeated the Italians.

However, the Ethiopian emperor, Haile Selassie, soon began to violate the act of federation. He increasingly interfered in the federal government's administration, banning Eritrean political parties and trade unions and replacing the major languages of Tigrinya and Arabic with Amharic, Ethiopia's official language. Within a decade the Selassie regime systematically annexed Eritrea, overwhelming its federal government and imposing the regime's own law in the federation.

Eritrea lost its federal status for good in 1962, becoming Ethiopia's 14th province. But the angry Eritrean people had no way to fight back. Protesters suffered at the hands of the police and were jailed or forced into exile. Getting outside help was impossible, as their head of state was Selassie's own son-in-law. The only solution seemed to be armed struggle, a reality Eritrea would face for the next 30 years.

The federation of Eritrea with Ethiopia was not enough to satisfy Emperor Haile Selassie's thirst for power.

FIGHT FOR FREEDOM

The Ethiopian regime in Eritrea razed villages, kidnapped and killed innocent people, jailed or exiled political leaders, drained economic resources, and displaced hundreds of thousands of people, many of whom sought refuge in neighboring Sudan.

In 1960 exiled Eritreans in Cairo formed the Eritrean Liberation Front (ELF) to raise arms against the Ethiopians. The ELF received enthusiastic support from disgruntled Eritrean workers and students, and soon the revolution spread to the central highlands in Eritrea. However, internal disagreements caused some members to withdraw and form another movement, which would later be named the Eritrean People's Liberation Front (EPLF).

Although the two fronts continued to fight one another—even when Selassie was overthrown in Ethiopia in 1974 and replaced by a new military dictator—they joined forces as a team and succeeded in freeing most of the Eritrean towns from Ethiopian grip. In fact they might have won control

THE ERITREAN PEOPLE'S LIBERATION FRONT

The first group to form against Ethiopian rule was the Eritrean Liberation Movement (ELM). Founded by young Eritreans exiled in Sudan, it attracted both Muslim and Christian Eritreans. With no clear plan, the ELM had a short life. In July 1960 exiled Eritreans in Egypt set up the Eritrean Liberation Front (ELF). This Muslim-dominated movement soon became the leader of the war against Ethiopian rule. To enable Christian Eritreans to join the armed struggle, the People's Liberation Front (PLF) was formed in 1971. A year later the Eritrean Liberation Force (another ELF) formed and merged with the PLF. The ELF-PLF coalition later became the Eritrean People's Liberation Front (EPLF), which took several towns back from the Ethiopians. The ELF had its fair share of military victories, but it withdrew in 1980, leaving the EPLF to fight the war alone. The EPLF fought unceasingly for another decade, emerging victorious in Asmara in 1991. Aside from securing military success, the group also embarked on a farsighted program to prepare the population for independence. While training youths in warfare (pictured below), EPLF leaders also taught them the banned Tigrinya language to preserve their heritage. Many Eritreans received their education this way. After independence the EPLF became the People's Front for Democracy and Justice (PFDJ), from which most of today's Eritrean leaders come.

over Eritrea, if not for the delivery of new armaments to Ethiopia in 1977 by the Soviet Union. Within a year the Ethiopian regime had regained most of Eritrea, and the ELF and the EPLF were forced to retreat and start again. Only the EPLF survived, fed by a steady flow of Eritreans eager to fight for their freedom. The EPLF fought the bloody war against Ethiopia for another decade, reclaiming Eritrea town by town. When the Soviet Union withdrew its military aid to Ethiopia in the late 1980s, Ethiopia fell. In May 1991 the EPLF assumed complete control over Eritrea.

INDEPENDENCE

When the residents of Asmara realized that the city had been liberated at 10:00 A.M. on May 24, 1991, they ran out of their houses and danced in the streets. For the first time in more than a hundred years, they were free.

The EPLF established a provisional government and held a national referendum in April 1993 to conclude the country's struggle for freedom. Almost everyone who voted chose independence, and on May 24, 1993, Eritrea

A groundskeeper makes his way past the graves of former fighters and soldiers at the Martyr's Cemetery in Asmara. The cruel liberation war has left a permanent scar on the Eritrean psyche.

was formally declared independent. Relations with Ethiopia started out smoothly, owing to the close friendship between the new Eritrean and Ethiopian leaders. As a gesture of goodwill, Eritrea guaranteed Ethiopian access to the Red Sea through the port of Assab. This privilege was later withdrawn when hostilities erupted over border disputes.

FOES ONCE AGAIN

In 1997 relations between the two neighbors soured when Ethiopia drew up a new map that placed parts of southwest Eritrea in Ethiopian territory. Fighting broke out as each side tried to capture the disputed land. A truce brokered by U.S. and Italian mediators halted the fighting at the end of 1998, but a few months later the two sides clashed again. In May 2000 Ethiopia occupied large parts of Eritrea and in June that year, both sides agreed to a ceasefire. A peace agreement was signed under the auspices of the United Nations in December. During the two-year war, more than a million Eritreans were displaced and 20,000 soldiers were killed.

Under the terms of the peace agreement, a 4,200-strong multinational peacekeeping force was deployed in the disputed area to monitor a 15.5-mile-wide (25-km-wide) Temporary Security Zone along the border. In 2002 the Permanent Court of Arbitration in The Hague published its decision on the border dispute, but Ethiopia declined to implement the decision without further negotiations, which the Eritreans rejected. Subsequently, in 2007, the Eritrea-Ethiopia Boundary Commission remotely demarcated the border by coordinates, leaving Ethiopia still occupying several tracts of disputed territory. Eritrea accepted the "virtual demarcation," but Ethiopia rejected it. The situation has still not been resolved.

Eritreans celebrating their country's independence. Of the 98.5 percent of eligible voters who cast their ballots in the national referendum in April 1993, 99.8 percent said "yes" to independence.

GOVERNMENT

Eritreans walking by the regional administration government building in Asmara. Eritrea is divided into six main regions (zobas).

THE NEWEST STATE IN AFRICA, *Hagere Ertra* (State of Eritrea) was proclaimed on May 24, 1993. To reflect the changed political conditions, the provisional government set up after liberation was reorganized into the People's Front for Democracy and Justice (PFDJ).

The PFDJ, now the only legal political party in the country, participates in the legislative branch of the democratic government of Eritrea. Known as the National Assembly, the legislature elects the president.

Eritrea's first and current president is Isaias Afwerki, who led the EPLF in its fight for independence. He and his cabinet of 17 ministers head the executive branch—the State Council—of the government. The State Council includes regional governors and other officials, who aid

This liberation monument features the original tanks that freed the city from the Ethiopian communist military junta.

the cabinet in implementing the policies and laws of the government. The judiciary consists of courts at national, regional, district, and village levels.

THE LEGISLATURE

The National Assembly outlines the domestic and foreign policies of the government, regulates the State Council's execution of these policies, approves the country's budget, and elects the president. It also ratifies the president's nominations of leaders for the various ministries, authorities, commissions, and offices.

Of the 150 seats in the legislature, 30 percent have been reserved for women to encourage female participation in governing the country. The PFDJ's Central Committee makes up half of the total membership, while the other half consists of representatives directly elected by the general population. Sixty of the latter come from the Constituent Assembly, which was set up to ratify the country's first constitution. The remaining 15 elected members represent Eritreans living abroad. Although national elections have not been held yet, local and regional elections take place on a regular basis.

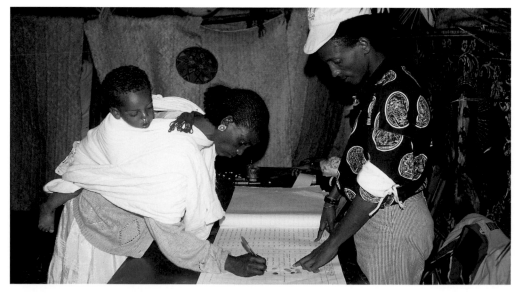

Voting is a new experience for this young nation.

THE CONSTITUTION

After gaining independence in 1993, the government set up a Constitutional Commission to draft Eritrea's first governmental constitution. To ensure the best possible constitution, the commission sought the views of as many Eritreans as possible, both at home and abroad. Even Eritrean refugees in Sudan were involved in the information-gathering process. The constitution was ratified in May 1997.

Refugees returning from Sudan. The views of these displaced Eritreans counted in the drafting of their country's first constitution.

The country's democratic constitution guarantees freedom of expression and equal rights for all Eritreans, regardless of gender, race, or religion. It also authorizes a multiparty system and allows any number of political parties to take part in elections, provided that they are not based on religious or ethnic foundations.

All Eritreans age 18 and above are entitled to vote in both regional and national elections. However, presidential and parliamentary elections due in 2001 were postponed indefinitely because of the outbreak of the border conflict with Ethiopia.

VOICES OF DISSENT

With the delay in holding national elections, dissatisfaction started to sweep some factions of the PFDJ, especially in view of what they considered President Afwerki's increasingly autocratic ways. In 2001 several prominent party members publicly called for elections and for the implementation of the constitution. Afwerki's response was to arrest 11 dissidents and hold them without charge. At the same time the government shut down the independent press and arrested several reporters and editors. Fourteen journalists remain jailed without having been formally charged.

In 2002 the National Assembly decided that the creation of political parties was not important for Eritrea, thus reaffirming the PFDJ as the only

The judiciary runs
civilian, military,
and special courts.

legal party in the country. A number of illegal parties and pressure groups operate both within and outside the country.

THE JUDICIARY

The judiciary is nominally independent of the legislative and executive arms of the government. The Ministry of Justice oversees a three-tier legal structure—the high court, regional courts and sub-regional courts, and community courts—that administers justice from the national level down to the villages.

The highest court is the High Court. The top judges are appointed by the president. Next come the city courts, which administer justice in the large cities. At the regional level there are 10 provincial courts and 29 district courts. Special Sharia courts cater to the Muslim population, following Islamic Sharia law in family cases.

The judiciary finds itself constantly subjected to interference from the legislative branch. In 2001 the president of the High Court was fired for criticizing the government for judicial interference.

INTERNAL ADMINISTRATION

Eritrea is divided into six regions, each of which has its own capital. Asmara is the capital city of both the central province and the entire country. Each region is further divided into subregions and towns.

Regional governors are mostly nominated by the president, and their appointment is ratified by the National Assembly. A governor oversees a team of local councillors, who are directly elected by the residents of their village or town. Regional elections held in 2002 chose 377 representatives. In local elections in 2004, 12,000 candidates made it to the local councils. Each council manages the daily running of a constituency and looks after the welfare of the residents.

Regional and local administration is often inefficient due to a lack of funds. Many local councils do not function properly because staff members are poorly trained.

NATIONAL SYMBOLS

The Eritrean flag is split into three triangles. Starting from the hoist edge, a horizontal red isosceles triangle divides the rest of the flag into two right triangles, the upper one being in green and the lower one in blue. A gold olive wreath is superimposed on the red section. The national flag is a combination of two other flags: the old Eritrean flag and the EPLF flag. The national flag draws the laurel olive symbol from its 1952—1959 predecessor and the colored triangles from the EPLF flag. The president's flag is similar to the new national flag, but with the country's national emblem in the place of the olive wreath. The national emblem is a camel encircled by an olive wreath.

The Eritrean currency is a national symbol in itself, having been named after the town of Nakfa, the location of the defense of the country's armed struggle against the Ethiopian regime throughout the late 1970s and 1980s.

The National Martyrs' Park is another potent national symbol. Dedicated on June 19, 1997, the eve of Martyrs' Day, it boasts more than 692 acres (280 hectares) of beautiful plains, valleys, and mountains in the highlands just southeast of Asmara. The Eritrean government views the park as the most important historical and natural resource to be passed from one generation to the next. Each tree in the park commemorates one of the 65,000 fighters and tens of thousands of civilians who lost their lives during the fight for freedom from Ethiopian rule. The park is a national enterprise, with every Eritrean, whether in the country or abroad, adopting a tree. It also features the National Martyrs' Monument, on which each martyr's name is engraved, and museums detailing the country's fight for independence. In Asmara, the Sandals (right) is another monument commemorating the victory of Eritrean fighters. This metal statue of a pair of giant sandals recalls the rubber sandals made from recycled tires, which the fighters wore to war.

NATIONAL SERVICE

Every Eritrean between the ages of 18 and 40, male or female, has to contribute to the country's welfare by performing 18 months of national service. Students who have completed secondary school undergo 6 months of military training and spend 10 months repairing roads or helping to educate illiterate adults. National service teams have constructed dams and wells, repaired roads, terraced hillsides to reduce erosion, and planted millions of tree seedlings.

Men between the ages of 18 and 40 and women between 18 and 27 serve in the military for 6 months at a place called Sawa. Eritrea has a big military sector, which includes an air force. The largest part of the military is the army, despite government efforts to demobilize the EPLF force. Eritrean troops are concentrated near the borders with Sudan and Ethiopia. The small navy protects the country's Red Sea coast and islands.

The Eritrean soldiers marching before an audience.

Although Eritrea has pledged to demobilize its civilian army, it has been slow to do so. At the height of the 1998—2000 border conflict with Ethiopia, nearly 300,000 soldiers were in service. It is estimated that nearly 1 in 20 Eritreans serves actively in the army.

INTERNATIONAL RELATIONS

Eritrea is a member of a number of international organizations, including the United Nations, the World Health Organization, the International Monetary Fund, the Organization for African Unity, and the African, Caribbean, and Pacific group of Third World countries that get preferential access to certain European Union markets. Eritrea also maintains friendly relations with several European countries—especially its former colonial ruler, Italy—and with the United States.

Eritrean president Isaias Afwerki (*right*) welcomes Sudan's president Omar Hassan al-Bashir (*left*) at the airport in Asmara.

Relations with the immediate neighbors, however, are not as healthy, mainly because of territorial disputes. Competition with Yemen over the Hanish Islands in the Red Sea was resolved with international arbitration in 1998. Also in 1998 the border conflict with Ethiopia flared into a war. Although a ceasefire went into effect in 2000, the dispute has not been resolved yet. A military confrontation took place along the border with Djibouti in 2008, and here too, relations remain strained. Eritrea normalized relations with Sudan in 2006, but accusations continue to fly between the two neighbors over each other's support for opposition forces in the other country.

Although Eritrea is in dire need of economic aid, the government practices great caution in accepting any form of help from other countries. It will flatly refuse offers that come with strings attached—unreasonable conditions that may endanger the young and fragile country's freedom. Neither does it favor aid from international nongovernmental organizations such as the Red Cross. Instead Eritreans remain steadfast in their desire to own their land, working proudly to become self-reliant and to build their country on their own.

ECONOMY

The government-owned Commercial Bank of Eritrea is the only banking institution in Eritrea that provides the full range of banking services.

CHAPTER 4

FROM NO EXTERNAL DEBT UPON independence, Eritrea now owes US$311 million. According to an International Monetary Fund (IMF) report of 2007 the country is not likely to be able to pay back its debt.

After a good start in the 1990s the Eritrean economy was battered by the border war with Ethiopia, combined with years of drought and the global economic crisis. In addition to these external factors, the government's restrictive policy only serves to exacerbate the country's economic problems. There is practically no private sector, with almost all sectors of the economy in the hands of PFDJ-owned companies,

In Eritrea, one of the world's poorest nations, each person lives on an average annual income of $700. This is less than half the figure for sub-Saharan Africa. Nearly half of the population lives below the poverty line.

Port machinery in operation at the port in Assab. Port activities contribute around half of the country's gross domestic product (GDP).

and foreign investment is almost nonexistent due to the government's tight control on foreign exchange. Today foreign exchange for the Eritrean economy comes mainly from annual remittances sent by its citizens living abroad. Migrants contribute about a third of the country's GDP through the money they send back.

Inflation is high, at around 20 percent in 2009, triggered by the rise in world food prices. Eritrea is the most expensive place in the world to buy fuel. In 2008, the country spent more than 8 percent of its GDP on fuel and food. After falling into negative territory in 2000, the GDP growth rate bounced back to reach 2.5 percent in 2009.

AGRICULTURE AND PASTORALISM

Nearly 80 percent of the Eritrean population depends on agriculture for a living, but this sector accounts for only about 12 percent of the GDP. Eritrea is not self-sufficient in food and even in good harvest years, it needs to import at least 40 percent of its food. Poor soils, erratic rainfall, and archaic cultivation methods hamper any attempt to increase agricultural yields. Nevertheless there is great potential for improvement. Of the 8 million acres (3.2 million ha) of arable land in the country, only 5 percent is cultivated. Soil erosion on the central plateau and severely depleted forest resources also present major challenges to the industry.

A woman gathers the harvest in a teff field near the town of Senafe.

A shepherd herds his flock of goats down a road in Keren.

Before World War II the Italian colonists set up large irrigated plantations that produced a variety of cash crops, but the war destroyed almost everything, and cultivation is now done mainly by subsistence farmers. These farmers produce food for their own use and a small surplus for trade.

Farmers in the highlands grow several types of traditional grain, such as teff, wheat, millet, barley, and corn. Teff looks like millet and contains yeast, which makes it rise. Being high in protein, complex carbohydrates, and minerals and low in fat, teff is an ideal food and is used to make the national staple *injera* (in-JEHR-uh). The main crops on the lowlands are sorghum, millet, and corn, though this region also supports the growing of vegetables and tropical fruits, such as papayas, bananas, and oranges. Plantations on the escarpment produce cotton, sesame, coffee, rubber, and tobacco.

Closely related to agriculture is pastoralism, another traditional Eritrean occupation. Pastoralists earn their living from animal husbandry, rearing goats, camels, sheep, and cattle for milk and meat. Some tribes, such as the nomadic Beja and Afar, consist mostly of shepherds, who wander through the pastoral lowlands with their herds according to weather conditions. Agriculturalists, on the other hand, settle in the highlands, but the two occupations are not mutually exclusive: Farmers may rear some animals, and shepherds may cultivate some grain.

FISHING

With a long coastline and vast territorial waters, fishing holds long-term prospects for the Eritrean economy. Species for exploitation include tuna, cuttlefish, crabs, parrotfish, oysters, and sea cucumbers. Commercial fishing is slowly turning from artisanal to industrial, and the country has started to export fish and sea cucumbers to Europe and Asia on a small basis. The Red Sea is still under-fished and could potentially provide an enormous source of revenue for the country. Eritrea could sustainably harvest around 77,000 tons (70,000 metric tons), but the current catch is around 14,300 tons (13,000 metric tons). Fishermen sell their catch to the National Fisheries Corporation that in turn sells it to processors such as Erifish.

A fisherman casts his net into the sea.

With the help of the United Nations, the Ministry for Marine Resources has put in place a Fisheries Development Project to maximize revenue from offshore fishing and fish processing, while protecting and preserving marine resources through nature reserves. The project funds the purchase of bigger boats and better fishing gear while educating fishermen on modern fishing techniques. Infrastructure such as jetties and boat repair plants have been built in several fishing communities, and a boat factory has been set up in Haleb. In addition plans are under way to organize the fishermen into an association.

INDUSTRY

Many of the big names in the Eritrean economy originated in the Italian colonial era, which saw a considerable rate of industrial expansion. Most of these factories were concentrated in Asmara, and they churned out food products, beer, tobacco, textiles, and leather goods. Eritrea soon acquired a reputation for producing shoes of good quality. The native workforce at that time learned skills that helped them find jobs abroad when they left their country during the war years.

Today contribution of manufacturing industries to exports is almost negligible, with leather being the main export product. Light industrial output consists primarily of foods, salt, textiles, and leather goods produced by both public and private small- to medium-scale enterprises located mainly in Asmara. Most of these factories are merely producing domestic substitutes for foreign products but are working to become more productive by modernizing facilities and training labor.

Heavy industry consists of salt and cement plants near Massawa. Potential sources of revenue are the two mines slated to open at Bisha by late 2010 and Zara in 2011. The rebuilding of the Massawa—Asmara railroad was one of the most demanding infrastructure projects in the country to date. Originally built by the Italians, the railroad was totally destroyed during the war for independence by Ethiopian soldiers, who used the rails to build trenches. Using the expertise of the original railroad builders and materials salvaged from the abandoned lines and trains, the Eritrean government completed the rebuilding in 2003 at a cost of just 5 percent of what was originally required to build the lines the first time around. With its capacity of 800,000 tons (725,748 metric tons) of freight a year, the railway provided a boost to the economy while becoming a tourist attraction itself.

Women working in a garment factory in Asmara.

A salt plain in the Danakil Depression in Eritrea. The salt here is harvested using the traditional method: The salt is scraped into small mounds for water evaporation and easier transportation, dried over fire, and finally enriched with iodine.

MINERALS

Eritrea has substantial deposits of many minerals. Salt is found in abundance. Vast salt flats lie like ice-covered lakes in the area around Assab, in Massawa, and in the Kobar Sink in the Danakil Depression. Salt mining is a traditional occupation for Eritreans living in the Southern Red Sea region. Miners dislodge slabs of solid salt during the dry season and sell the crude blocks at the markets in Assab and Massawa.

Other commercially viable minerals found in the country are the metallic ores of gold, silver, copper, zinc, lead, and iron, and industrial minerals, such as sulfur, feldspar, gypsum, silica, and potash. Of these gold shows the best prospects. The mining industry is set to create a veritable boom in the country, with about 20 international companies having bought a stake in the industry. In addition deposits of granite, marble, slate, and limestone can be quarried for use in the construction industry.

The proximity of the oil-rich Arabian Peninsula has raised hopes of finding petroleum in Eritrean territory. Although efforts since the days of Italian rule have been unproductive, surveys have indicated the presence of oil and natural gas deposits in the Red Sea. The government has signed exploration deals with several companies since the 1990s, the latest to date being London-based Centric Energy Corporation. Although President Afwerki has recently implied that oil has been discovered in great quantities, exploitation has not started.

ERITREAN MONEY

The Eritrean currency is the nakfa *(Nkfa). One nakfa equals 100 cents. Notes come in denominations of 1, 5, 20, 50, and 100 nakfa, and coins come in denominations of 1, 5, 10, 25, 50, and 100 cents. One side of the notes depicts children and young women, while the reverse side has scenes from various parts of the country. The introduction of the nakfa as the Eritrean currency in 1997 was a double disappointment for Ethiopia. Besides replacing the Ethiopian* birr *that was formerly used in Eritrea, the new currency went by the name of the town where the Ethiopian army had sustained the most casualties. For Eritreans, however, the town of Nakfa represents freedom and happiness.*

TRADE

Eritrea has an extremely unfavorable balance of trade, importing much more than it can export. Moreover it exports mostly low-value goods, while importing expensive products. In 2009 the country exported an estimated US$12 million worth of livestock, sorghum, textiles, foods, and small consumer products. The same year Eritrea imported processed goods, machinery, and petroleum products to a total worth of about US$590 million, a staggering 50 times more than what it earned.

Eritrea's largest foreign market is India, which absorbs more than one-fourth of Eritrea's exports. Other destinations for Eritrean goods include Sudan, Italy, Saudi Arabia, China, and Yemen. The country's main source of foreign exchange is in the form of remittances from migrants in Europe and the United States. Eritrea spends a great deal of money on imports from Saudi Arabia, mainly on petroleum products. India is also a valuable import partner as well as Italy, China, and the United States.

When Eritrea became independent, Ethiopia absorbed all of its external debt. Today, however, the country is heavily in debt.

The railroad, such as this one from Asmara to Massawa, is the most reliable mode of interstate travel.

TRANSPORTATION AND COMMUNICATION

A strategic location on the Red Sea endows Eritrea with the natural potential to be a communications hub for northeastern Africa. The ports of Massawa and Assab serve as gateways to many of the neighboring lands. Direct access to an international shipping route extends Eritrea's reach to regional and global markets. Global transportation and communication is also possible from Asmara. An airport and telephone service equips the Eritrean capital with international connections. Another international airport 8.2 miles (13 km) northwest of Massawa opened in 2003. Although few airlines operate from Massawa, the airport serves as an alternative landing spot for Asmara-bound flights that need to be diverted due to bad weather. The third Eritrean international airport is at Assab. The national carrier is Eritrean Airlines.

Improving internal transportation and communication networks is a priority for the government. Telephones are available in the major towns, but national penetration is low. The system is improving but at a much slower rate than in the rest of Africa. Mobile phones were introduced in 2003 and are quite common in the towns. Combined fixed line and mobile subscribership was only 3 per 100 persons in 2008.

The Eritrean railway system runs along 190.5 miles (306.4 km), stretching from the port city of Massawa to Agordat via the capital city, Asmara. Reopened in 2003 it provides scheduled trips along some stretches where there is a demand. The system is currently being extended to the Bisha mine and on to the Sudanese border. Paved roads linking the major towns are in generally good condition. Intercity buses have no fixed timetable and depart only when they are filled. Long journeys break once or twice along the way for refreshments and visits to the restroom. Children ride free and share a seat with their adult companion.

There are buses in the major towns, but Eritreans tend to walk a lot. Asmara also has a fleet of minibuses and shared taxis catering to the commuting needs of residents. Rural transportation often features camels and donkeys.

ECONOMIC OPPORTUNITIES

The Eritrean government does not believe in accepting handouts from rich countries or nongovernmental organizations. It prefers to attract long-term foreign investment to build domestic infrastructure and thus facilitate economic recovery. Having identified tourism as a potential growth area, the government has established a 20-year tourism plan, entitled the 2020 Eritrea Tourism Development Plan, with the aim of conserving and enhancing the country's natural and cultural resources, boosting economic development, and reducing poverty. The Ministry of Tourism also actively takes part in tourism fairs in Europe and North America.

The Eritrean government is aware that the way to economic development is through foreign investment, and the Eritrea Investment Center mediates between foreign investors and the relevant government ministries. In order to attract international companies to the country, an appealing package of incentives is in place, including tax breaks and favorable tariffs. In addition, two free trade zones have been set up in Asmara and Massawa.

The 45-mile (72-km) Asmara-Massawa Cableway took two years to build and required 4,299 tons (3,900 metric tons) of cables and other materials. Powered by eight stations and traveling at 5.6 miles per hour (9 km per hour), its 1,620 trolleys transports 720 tons (653 metric tons) of cargo every day.

The Dahlak Hotel stands along the waterfront in Massawa.

ENVIRONMENT

The tranquil blue waters of the
Red Sea from Massawa in Eritrea.

CHAPTER 5

E RITREA FACES MANY environmental challenges today, brought about by the long war with Ethiopia, population pressures, as well as the needs of development.

However, well before the start of the struggle, the various colonial powers had started to lay waste to the country. In many parts the Eritrean landscape is desolate and harsh, leaving the population to scratch a meager living out of the scorched earth. Long stretches of drought have turned vast areas into desert wasteland.

But it was not always like this. In ancient times Eritrea was renowned as a land of plenty, with nearly every species of African mammal roaming the land. Nowadays many species have become extinct, and those still present find their habitat shrinking.

Women waiting on line for water in Adishekain.

"One day we hope renewable energy will meet 30 percent of our country's electricity requirements."
—Semere Habtezion, Director of the Division of Energy in the Ministry of Mines

It is imperative that the fragile environment be, if not redeemed, at least preserved. The Eritrean government finds itself in a difficult position, having to balance protection of the environment with the needs of the population.

NATURAL VEGETATION

Forests cover 3,916,000 acres (1,585,000 ha) or 13.5 percent of the total land area. The largest stretch of natural forest remaining in Eritrea is the Green Belt Zone, northeast of Asmara. Covering an extensive area along the eastern slope of the Central Plateau, it is lush and green because its two rainy seasons provide the zone with more than 39 inches (100 cm) of rain a year. The main vegetations at the higher levels are evergreens such as junipers and acacia, while shrubs and climbers predominate at the lower elevations.

The Central Plateau is also covered with junipers mixed with tropical species such as the African wild olive. Due to variations in rainfall and temperatures, vegetation is quite varied. Large tracts of forest have been cleared for agriculture.

The cactus-dotted rocky landscape of Eritrea.

The Western Escarpment has poor soil and is the habitat of scattered shrub-like acacia species and closed canopy woodland.

The two lowland areas are very different from each other. The Southwestern Lowland Zone is a fertile region of grassland interspersed with acacia and doum palm trees. Ficus and jujubes grow along the river banks. The Northwestern Lowland Zone, on the other hand, only supports semi-arid species such as the acacia scrub.

Mangroves cover an area of 29 square miles (75 square km) running along 236 miles (380 km) on the Red Sea coast. Dense mangrove forests are found near Assab and in patches around Tio, as well as around some offshore islands. The dominant species is the white mangrove that can grow to a height of 32 feet (10 m). On the northern side of the coastline, the Asiatic mangrove is also common. Yellow mangrove also occurs along the coast, but in smaller quantity.

Endangered plant species include the eucalyptus, baobab, frankincense tree, Egyptian balsam, sea lemon, and the tamarind tree.

DEFORESTATION

One of the greatest threats to the Eritrean environment is deforestation. From 30 percent a century ago, forest cover has shrunk to just over 13 percent. Since Italian colonization, large tracts of land have been cleared for agriculture. Today farmers are still converting forested land into fields for the production of food grain. As the population increases, more land is needed to grow food. Unfortunately yields are low because of poor methods of production and lack of expertise. Moreover, because the traditional land tenure system allows farmers the use of fields for a number of years only, there is no incentive to maintain the quality of the soil, resulting in poor soil condition. At the same time grasslands suffer from overgrazing, since more cattle are reared for the growing population. To make matters worse Eritrea has experienced a steady decline in rainfall since the 1940s, leading to long periods of drought.

During the 30-year war with Ethiopia, both sides cut down trees. The Eritrean army needed the wood for building trenches as well as for cooking purposes. The Ethiopians, on the other hand, uprooted thousands of trees to destroy the cover they provided for the Eritrean soldiers.

The main cause of deforestation today is the cutting of trees for fuel. In a country where the price of fuel is prohibitively high and electricity does not reach every household, wood fire is the fuel of choice for cooking. Most households, even those in Asmara, use wood-burning stoves to cook all meals. Firewood represents more than 70 percent of the total energy consumption of the country, with most of the fuel wood coming from the western lowlands. Substituting dung and crop residues for fuel only serves to exacerbate the problem because the nutrients from dung and residues are not going back to the soil, thus causing land degradation.

Ultimately deforestation leads to soil erosion and desertification. Land degradation in Eritrea has reached an alarming level, resulting in a dramatic decline in agricultural yield levels. However, deforestation is not the only cause of land degradation. Ironically certain trees have an adverse effect on the environment. The eucalyptus tree, introduced from Australia more than a century ago, is grown extensively in the highlands for firewood.

A truck filled with wood in Keren.

Unfortunately its long roots cover large areas and consume large amounts of underground water. Cacti behave in the same way, causing the soil to dry up in the long run. The worst culprit is the Temer-Musa, which appeared in Eritrea in the early 1990s. Spreading at a fast rate, it absorbs almost all the underground water and exterminates all plants around it.

Locals plant mangrove seeds in a village in Eritrea. These mangrove seeds help to provide feed to raise livestock and combat desertification.

MANGROVES TO THE RESCUE

Since the mid-1990s the village of Hirgigo on the Red Sea has been the site of an almost miraculous regeneration of habitat. Squeezed between barren mountains and the sea, this little desert village is a most unlikely place to witness such rejuvenation. The region is one of the hottest in the world, with temperatures soaring above 104°F (40°C) throughout the year and an average annual rainfall of just 1 inch (2 cm).

Started by American biochemist Dr. Gordon Sato, the Manzanar Project aims to improve the lives of desert coastal communities by using mangroves to increase fish production and combat desertification. Mangroves used to grow along the shore in Hirgigo, but most of it was cut down for firewood or to build huts. The rest was destroyed by overgrazing by camels. Replacing the mangrove trees prevents coastal erosion as the strong roots keep the

African elephants in the wild. These African elephants are larger than Asian elephants and both the males and females have tusks.

soil from being washed away. The mangrove forest also acts as an ecosystem for the fish, crabs, shrimps, and oysters, thus providing food for the village. The tree itself is a source of food—excess leaves and seeds are fed to sheep and goats—while dry branches are used as firewood.

Today tall mangrove trees stretch over 4 miles (7 km) of coast, growing 330 feet (100 m) deep. So far more than a million trees have been planted. This green band has had a massive impact on the community of about 3,000 people. Many women are employed to plant seeds and collect leaves, whereas the men go out to fish and sell their catch. Not only has the fish population grown in quantity, but also they are bigger in size.

In a region where water is a luxury, using salt water to plant trees provides a lifeline for the village community. Going one step further, Dr. Sato's team has been able to plant mangroves in areas where the trees did not exist previously. To do this low-cost slow-release fertilizer packs of nitrogen, phosphorus, and iron are planted alongside each seed so that it will receive all the nutrients essential for growth. This project opens up immense possibilities for desert coastal areas where food production is very difficult.

ANIMALS IN PERIL

A major consequence of deforestation is the decline in animal species as their natural habitat is destroyed. Every type of large game of the East African savannah was present in Eritrea as recently as in the mid-20th century. Today only gazelles, antelopes, leopards, zebras, hyenas, and monkeys can be seen in large numbers. The giraffe, rhinoceros, and hippo no longer roam the country. The Abyssinian wild ass is critically endangered, with fewer than 500 living on the coastal plains. Even fewer in numbers is the African elephant.

Between 1955 and 2001 there were no sightings at all and the elephant was thought to have gone extinct. However, in December 2001, a herd of about 30 was spotted near the Gash River. Today there are about 100 elephants left in Eritrea. As for the lion, it is reported to live in southwestern Gash Barka, but there has been no confirmed sighting in more than 20 years.

Among the small mammals, the painted hunting dog is extinct, but foxes and jackals are quite plentiful. Baboons live in the highlands, where they need cliffs to sleep. Hares, mongoose, badgers, and aardvarks can be encountered in areas with high human populations.

More than 570 species of birds make their nest in Eritrea, with nearly 20 endemic species. As the country lies on one of the major migration routes into Africa, large numbers of raptors pass through. Within Africa, the white-collared kingfisher is only found in Eritrea. It breeds in the coastal mangrove forests. The Dahlak Islands are important breeding sites for a number of sea and shore birds, including the white-eyed gull (33 percent of the world population), the crab plover (20 percent of the world population), and several terns and boobies. The Socotra cormorant, which also breeds in the southern islands, is a threatened species.

THE RED SEA

Famed for its marine diversity, the Red Sea supports the highest degree of native species in the world. At least 17 percent of the 1,400 species of fish and 20 percent of the 250 coral species recorded here are found nowhere else on the Earth. Eritrea's coastal waters have a favorable climatic condition for reef growth, with warm waters and low rainfall. Here coral exists mainly as patch reef, extending from the surface to a depth of about 50 feet (15 m). A smaller amount of fringing reef can also be found. Reef formation is stronger around the island coastlines, whereas the reefs along the mainland coastline are less developed mainly due to sedimentation from the rivers' runoff. The most pristine reefs occur in the Dahlak Archipelago. Although Eritrean corals have not suffered from any major disaster in the past few decades, the Red Sea marine environment is highly susceptible to pollution, mainly because of its small size and limited oceanographic circulation.

Despite being legally protected in many countries, dugong numbers are dwindling due to hunting, habitat degradation or loss, and commercial fishing.

The waters off the coast of Eritrea support a wide variety of marine wildlife, with 600 resident species of fish. The most common reef fish are the colorful surgeonfish, wrasse, snapper, angelfish, and grouper. The whale shark and manta ray also patrol the waters. Four species of whale live in the Red Sea, of which the Bryde's whale and the sperm whale are endangered. Four species of dolphin are also frequently seen in Eritrean waters. Although it is distributed over a wide area, the bottle-nosed dolphin is a protected species. Fishing communities do consume the meat of dolphins if they are caught accidentally and die in nets. In addition, the skin of the dolphin is used to produce a type of oil, which is valued for its medicinal properties. The dugong, a shy marine mammal also called a "sea cow," finds a very favorable habitat among the sea grasses of the Red Sea. It lives in pairs or small groups in the shallow coastal waters of Eritrea. Worldwide the dugong is believed to be near extinction, with Eritrean waters holding at least half of the 4,000 animals that live in the Red Sea. They sometimes get trapped in fishermen's nets or wash up dead on beaches.

Five of the world's seven turtle species breed in Eritrea. They are the hawksbill, olive ridley, loggerhead, leatherback, and green turtle. The mainland coastline, as well as some of the larger islands, provide good nesting grounds for greens, hawksbills, and olive ridleys. All five species are threatened with extinction. Despite official bans and educational measures, the coastal population still consumes turtle products, mainly eggs and meat. Turtles are also caught in the nets of fish trawlers.

LANDMINES

Eritrea ranks second behind Angola on the list of the worst landmine-affected countries in Africa. During the country's long struggle for independence and again when it was at war with Ethiopia, thousands of landmines were laid by both sides. A survey completed in 2004 identified 914 suspected hazardous areas covering approximately 50 square miles (129 square km) in total. The problem is almost nationwide, with areas in the north of the country and the highlands affected as much as those in the disputed border zone. In the latter region both antipersonnel and antivehicle mines pose a great danger. Mines were used to defend strongholds around cities and populated areas, military camps and roads, and near water sources.

A mine clearing demonstration from the Eritrean Demining Authority in Asmara educates locals about the dangers of landmines.

A total population of 655,000 living in 481 communities is socially and economically affected by mines and unexploded ordnance. Most people at risk are rural inhabitants, nomadic people, internally displaced persons, and refugees. Landmines not only cause physical injury to humans and animals, but they also destroy the environment. More than half of the disabled people in Eritrea are landmine survivors, making landmines the most important cause of physical disability in the country.

The Eritrean government agreed to the Mine Ban Treaty in 2001. Under the terms of the treaty, the country must destroy all antipersonnel mines in mined areas under its jurisdiction or control by February 1, 2012, at the latest. With the help of various United Nations agencies, the Eritrean Demining Authority has embarked on a program of technical survey, marking, and clearance so that refugees can return home. Mine risk education is also carried out in schools and communities. Local populations are taught to recognize landmines and other weapons and to avoid contact with them.

MINING

Eritrean soil is rich in base metals and gold, and exploration activities have confirmed that prospects for the mining industry are excellent. The country is sitting on a potential hoard of several billion pounds of zinc, millions of pounds of copper, as well as millions of ounces of gold and silver.

The Bisha mine is Eritrea's first new mine since colonial times. Operated by a joint venture between the Eritrean government and a Canadian company, Bisha is slated to start production in late 2010. Over a period of 10 years the mine west of Asmara is expected to yield 1.06 million ounces (30 million grams) of gold, 10 million ounces (283.4 million g) of silver, 747 million pounds (339 million kg) of copper, and more than one billion pounds (453.6 million kg) of zinc. Another mine, operated by an Australian firm, Chalice Gold Mines, will open in Zara in the north of the country in 2011.

The Eritrean government views the mining industry as the new motor for its needy economy. With a free 10 percent stake in all mining ventures as well as an option to buy another 30 percent, the government is set to reap unprecedented benefits. On top of that the company pays a 38 percent tax on net income.

The downside of the mining industry is that it leads to the degradation of the environment. The open-pit operation in use in Bisha is ecologically harmful as it requires the clearing of large tracts of land and creates pollution. The indigenous population is displaced and their lifestyle inexorably changed.

CONSERVATION MEASURES

The Eritrean government has put in place a vast program of environmental recovery, beginning with reforestation of the denuded hillside catchment area. Immediately after independence a tree planting campaign encountered great success, especially from students and the army. The Ministry of Agriculture has now turned its attention to the conservation of woodlands and wildlife. A total ban on the cutting of live trees, hunting or capture of wildlife, and charcoal making is in force. Adapted from an old tradition practiced by the local communities, the government policy of forest closure enables the natural vegetation to regenerate successfully. "Temporary closure" is carried out for a limited period of time, from a few months to a few years. "Permanent closure" creates favorable conditions for vegetation recovery, protects endangered flora and wildlife, controls runoff and loss of arable land by erosion, and increases infiltration for water conservation and for more soil moisture. The Semenawi Bahri National Park, north of Asmara, is an example of permanent closure.

The other national park in the country is the Dahlak Marine National Park in the Red Sea. The waters around the Dahlak Islands teem with fish and corals. Scuba diving is strictly regulated, and visitors require a permit to enter the area. In 2006 Eritrea announced that it would become the first country in the world to turn its entire coast into an environmentally protected zone. With the support of the United Nations Environment Program (UNEP), the Eritrea Coastal, Marine and Islands Biodiversity (ECMIB) Project conducts seminars and other educational programs to raise awareness among coastal communities of the need to protect marine turtles. For example the ECMIB Project Turtle Team has started a sea turtle club in the town of Assab, in collaboration with the National Union of Eritrean Youth and Students (NUEYS) in order to teach the children of fishermen about conservation measures.

Women compacting soil in seedbags at the tree nursery in the countryside of Eritrea. Replanting trees and shrubs is a national priority for the country.

ERITREANS

An Eritrean mother and her wide-eyed child.

E RITREA HAS A SMALL POPULATION of almost 6 million people. A vast displacement of Eritreans occurred in the 1960s and 1970s, with many families taking refuge in neighboring Sudan and Saudi Arabia as well as far away in North America and Europe.

Most Eritreans who sought refuge in the West have set up permanent homes there. They now constitute Eritrea's diaspora. Although many Eritreans who fled to Sudan have returned, a significant number still await repatriation.

From 2005 onward the population has grown consistently at a rate of around 2.5 percent. However there are still many infant deaths, and the average life span is only about 62 years.

Smiling children at a school in Eritrea.

Eritreans are a diverse people, with many languages, cultures, and religions. Nine main ethnic groups inhabit different parts of the country, but they live in relative unity. Ethnic friction is thus almost nonexistent, and the constitution allows no discrimination against any group. Today Eritreans show solidarity in their desire to develop their country.

TIGRINYA

The 2.5 million Tigrinya people in Eritrea make up about half the country's total population. Living in the southern highlands, they speak Tigrinya and most of them are Christian. Being the descendants of early Semitic settlers in the Horn of Africa, the Tigrinya are related to the Sabean people who claim to be descended from the biblical Queen of Sheba. One of their historical achievements was setting up the ancient empire of Aksum. The Eritrean Tigrinya people share this ancient heritage with the 4 million inhabitants of the Ethiopian region of Tigray.

A Tigrinya man. The Tigre-Tigrinya people are descendants of early Semitic-speaking people living in the region spanning central Eritrea and northern Ethiopia.

The Tigrinya are a group of beautiful and hardworking people whose determination contributed significantly to their country's attainment of freedom. Today they are helping to build Eritrea with the same perseverance. Their spirit of sacrifice is also noteworthy, and they are likely to go hungry and offer their food to others who need it more.

The Tigrinya people are mostly peasants cultivating vegetables and grain in the temperate highlands. Drinking coffee constitutes an important part of their social life, and the women have a strong penchant for jewelry. The Tigrinya people also have a rich heritage in music, featuring drums and string instruments.

TIGRE

Numbering more than 1.1 million, the Tigre constitute the second-largest ethnic group in Eritrea. Although they go by a similar-sounding name, the Tigre people are different from the Tigrinya: The Tigre are descendants of the ancient Egyptians, profess the Muslim faith, and lead nomadic lifestyles.

Scattered in the northern highlands and on the eastern and western lowlands, many Tigre have gradually moved to Sudan in search of water and pastures. Traditionally being a nomadic tribe, they roam the countryside with their herds of goats, sheep, cattle, and camels, which they sell in the markets when they need to buy other essential items. A small number of the Tigre are farmers. Living in round huts with cone-shaped roofs, they cultivate corn, sorghum, wheat, barley, and legumes for food. Many Tigre people depend on government aid to support their large families.

A Tigre family may offer a daughter in marriage to a man from another Tigre family to resolve a feud between the two families that would otherwise end in bloodshed.

Young Tigre women in their traditional outfits.

AFAR

More than 200,000 Eritreans of the Afar tribe live in the southern desert plains of the country. They are also known as the Danakil, after the region in which they live, but this term offends them. They claim their ancestry in Noah and are a proud and strong people known for being ferocious warriors. In his book *The Danakil Diary*, Wilfred Thesiger said that "no Danakil man may wear a colored loincloth, a comb or feather in his hair, nor decorate his knife with brass or silver until he has killed at least one [lion]."

Nearly all Afar are Muslims. They are divided into two subgroups. The "red ones" (as translated from their language) are the powerful nobles living along the coast, while the "white ones" are the commoners living in the mountains and in the Danakil Desert.

The Afar build oval-shaped huts from palm mats and set up camps surrounded by thorn barricades to protect them from wild animals and enemy tribes. Most of the Afar are nomads who herd sheep, goats, cattle, and camels. The size of their herds indicates their wealth. Some of the Afar near the Red Sea coast make their living as fishermen as well.

Although some Afar have adopted an urban lifestyle, the majority have remained nomadic pastoralists.

The Afar have traditionally traveled beyond Eritrea into Ethiopian and Djibouti territory, where another 1.75 million Afar live. However, disputes between Eritrea and neighboring countries over national borders have had a negative effect on the Afar's nomadic way of life. Much of the disputed land includes their traditional routes of travel.

BEJA

Being an ancient people scattered across the desert regions of Eritrea, Egypt, and Sudan, the Beja consider themselves descendants of Noah's grandson, Cush. Numbering around 3 million altogether, the Beja are the largest non-Arabic ethnic group between the Nile River and the Red Sea, and they have settled in the region for over 4,000 years. More than 200,000 Beja inhabit approximately 20,000 square miles (51,800 square km) in the western plain in Eritrea. Thousands of Eritrean Beja were driven into Sudan during the war.

The Beja were the powerful people in ancient times. Having established their kingdom in all of Eritrea after the fall of the Aksumite Empire, they are in a sense the common ancestor of all Eritreans living today, although many of the later generations do not trace their roots to the original Beja.

There are two Beja tribes in Eritrea: the Hedareb and the Beni-Amer. These tribes are made up of clans varying in size from 1 to 12 families. The Hedarab live in the far north of the country and manifest a strong Arab influence. The Beni-Amer have developed a social system that resembles a caste system and that the government strongly discourages.

With small, strong, and wiry frames, long noses, and oval faces, today's Beja people are semi-nomadic shepherds who live in portable tents built by the women. They are Muslims and speak the Beja language. Many are also fluent in Arabic or Tigre. Male children are highly favored among young Beja couples.

A Beja nomad woman holding her child.

ETHNIC MINORITIES

The Nara, Kunama, Bilen, Saho, and Rashaida make up about 12 percent of the Eritrean population. Many minority groups belong to the Muslims faith. They live in most parts of the country, except in the central highlands. The Nara and Kunama live in the western lowlands. The Bilen are mostly pastoralists who live in the northern highlands, mainly around Keren. The Saho reside on the coastal plain south of Massawa, quite close to the Afar. The Rashaida roam the northern hills and are the only true nomads in Eritrea. A small group of Nigerians lives near Teseney. Their ancestors settled there on the way to or from the Muslim holy city of Mecca in Saudi Arabia. Ethiopians, mostly of Tigrinya heritage, form a small and dwindling minority in Eritrea's ethnic mosaic.

The Rashaida are people of Arab origin.

WOMEN

Of the 65,000 fighters killed during the war with Ethiopia, one-third were women. Women made up 35 percent of the 95,000-strong EPLF army. Many of them fought at the front line during the liberation war, while those who stayed in the villages took over the jobs and roles of the men who had left to fight.

Returning from the war, however, Eritrean women saw their status decline. Some female fighters were considered unmarriageable when they returned to their native villages. Their independence and modern ways clashed with the traditional rural lifestyle. Many village families consider their daughters farm and home laborers, and keep them out of school. Although women head more than 50 percent of households in some areas, they are often barred from agricultural activities because cultural norms prevent them from farming. Gender equality is enshrined in the constitution, but in reality women have a lower status both in the home and in the community. In addition Muslim women are governed by the Sharia law, which does not give them much protection. Female genital mutilation is still practiced in many communities and violence against women is widespread, particularly domestic violence and wife beating.

Eritrean perceptions of women are slowly changing with the example of female pioneers. Tirhas Iyassu, one of the best female painters in the country, paints images of men looking after children or cooking, to promote gender equality. The National Union of Eritrean Women is a semi-autonomous nongovernmental organization dedicated to improving the status of Eritrean women. With a membership of more than 200,000, the group aims to enhance the role of women by raising their political consciousness through literacy campaigns, credit programs, English language lessons, and other skills training.

The Eritrean government recognizes the role of women in national development and guarantees 30 percent of seats in national and regional elections to women. President Afwerki has appointed three female ministers in his cabinet, and there are women holding other senior government positions as well.

THE DIASPORA

Displaced Eritreans staying in a refugee camp.

The diaspora is a very important concept to Eritreans. It refers, in the collective, to all Eritreans who live outside their home country. Most of them escaped during the long 30-year war with Ethiopia. About 850,000 Eritreans reside in faraway countries, such as Australia, Canada, the United States, and Sweden. Virtually every family in Eritrea has at least one member living outside the country. Although members of the diaspora may have decided to settle permanently in their host countries, they still consider themselves Eritrean and raise their children with an Eritrean cultural awareness.

After liberation, many among the diaspora returned to Eritrea to help in its recovery, while others decided to stay in their host countries and help their home country in an indirect way. The latter regularly send money back to Eritrea, contributing substantially to the country's annual revenue. These worker remittances form a large and stable flow of income, without which the government would face even greater difficulty in implementing its massive infrastructural reconstruction program. Today many Eritreans who left the country as young children come back as tourists, to visit aged relatives and commune with the country of their birth. Some parents also send their foreign-born children back to Eritrea, so that they can experience hardship and not take life for granted.

One group that would like to return, if they had the means, are the Eritrean maids who go to Italy for work. Although they usually only earn a humble salary, many often send money back to Eritrea to help their families, or raise funds through activities such as the Bologna Festival.

THE REFUGEE PROBLEM

Around 750,000 Eritreans had to leave the country during the liberation war. Half a million people went to neighboring Sudan, 75,000 went to the Middle East, and 25,000 went to Europe and the United States. Most had to battle inhuman conditions in order to reach safety. By traveling at night on camel back or even on foot, many families fled to Sudan or Djibouti. Parents sent their children away to protect them from abuse by the Ethiopians or from conscription into the guerrilla army.

The refugees in Sudan lived in overcrowded camps with very few amenities. Life there was harsh, but far better than the life they had left behind in Eritrea. In the camps in Sudan each family had a hut with a little land to cultivate. The refugees organized their own communities, running schools for their children and rearing animals and crops for food. They earned a salary if they held a job inside or outside the camps. The women formed self-help groups to make handicrafts, which they sold for money. The more educated refugees even managed to find sponsors, usually from Christian organizations, to finance their migration to the West.

When the EPLF liberated most of the country in 1989, Eritrean refugees immediately began to return home by the thousands. The Commission for Eritrean Refugee Affairs managed the repatriation process and reintegrated the returnees into Eritrean society. Between 1989 and 1992 more than 80,000 refugees returned to Eritrea, with 80 percent coming from Sudan. This sudden influx was a strain on the new country. Housing and social services were overstretched. There were not enough work opportunities for all the returnees, many of whom did not have the necessary skills to help the country develop economically. The government instituted a plan to educate former refugees to help them get a job or start a business. Those with good business plans can apply for low-interest loans from the government to finance their start-up. While former fighters make up the new political class, returnees have taken over the economy of the country, going into business and setting up new enterprises.

Nearly 20 years after independence, the refugee problem has not been completely resolved. More than 100,000 Eritreans are still awaiting repatriation from camps in Sudan, and thousands are leaving the country each year to avoid conscription and to escape the repressive regime of President Afwerki. Today Eritrean refugees can be found in Ethiopia, Sudan, Egypt, Uganda, and Israel as well as in Europe and North America.

LIFESTYLE

A busy street in Asmara.

MANY ERITREANS LEAD LIFESTYLES that have changed little since biblical times. Many tribes still live as nomads, almost untouched by Western civilization, and follow ancient customs and traditions.

A wide divide exists in the way people live, especially between the urban and rural areas of Eritrea. In the past decade there have been massive reconstruction projects in the urban areas, in a bid to catch up with the rest of the world economically.

An Emergency and Recovery Action Program budgeted at close to US$2.5 billion was introduced after independence to develop the country's devastated transportation, agriculture, and industry sectors.

The construction of modern housing projects in Asmara.

An Eritrean farming family with their livestock.

Nevertheless both Asmara and Massawa still retain an Old World feel with their well-preserved buildings and slow pace of life. Asmara is one of the safest, cleanest, and most attractive capital cities in Africa. In the rural areas people struggle to eke out a living from meager resources.

Many survive only with government aid. The government aims to equip every child in the country with a basic education and to improve living conditions in most areas by installing basic facilities, such as piped water and electricity.

THE ERITREAN FAMILY

An Eritrean woman bears, on average, 4.6 children in her lifetime. But not all of her offspring survive to adulthood. The high birth rate balances the high infant mortality rate and short life expectancy. Nevertheless the Eritrean family remains relatively large by Western standards.

The father is the head of the household and the main breadwinner. If he loses the capacity to perform this role, his family is considered cursed. The mother feeds the family and does the household chores, usually with her daughters' help. Women and girls do all the laborious jobs, such as tending the vegetable garden. They sometimes walk more than two hours each day to bring water home from the well.

Both father and mother rarely play with their sons and daughters. However, they do tell their children traditional stories and teach them the names of their ancestors to pass on their cultural heritage. The mother showers her children with love and care, while the father is the disciplinarian and spends little time with his children. Eritrean men do not relish having daughters, as girls are less valued than boys in their society. However, the father—daughter relationship is safe from the tension that tends to build up between the father and a son who tries to assert himself.

Many children in Eritrea lost both their parents to the liberation war. Most of them live with their relatives, supported by a little financial aid from the government. In urban centers most young people are marrying late, taking time to enjoy their newfound freedom and occupying themselves with hobbies and sports. In traditional communities, however, girls barely out of childhood are married off, and sometimes they are married to men old enough to be their fathers. Some Muslim ethnic groups also practice polygamy.

Every Eritrean has a first name, by which he or she is known, followed by the father's name, which women keep even after marriage.

A Tigre hut is round with a cone-shaped roof made from palm mats.

LIFE IN THE VILLAGE

Over 75 percent of Eritreans live in the countryside. They generally build small huts out of stones, clay, and palm leaves. These can last up to 10 years if the palm is of good quality. On average it takes four men to build a hut in one day. The shape of the hut and the materials used vary slightly according to the location, lifestyle, and heritage of the tribe. A Nara village, for example, looks like a colony of beehives, as the roofs of the huts reach to the ground. Each Nara family has three huts: One is for the males, one is for the females, and one is used as a kitchen.

Rural life is slow and peaceful, keeping with the pace of nature in the raising of crops and livestock, but it is not an easy life. The people work hard to grow enough grain and vegetables, and to raise enough sheep and cattle to feed themselves, and the periodic droughts and famines bring great suffering. Still there are occasions to celebrate, such as weddings and major festivals, when the whole village comes together in ritualistic ceremonies.

Many Eritrean women dress in long, flowing, colorful dresses. A light shawl covers their head and drapes around their shoulders. Many Tigrinya women wear their traditional dress to festival celebrations and at their wedding. This long, white gown is embellished with golden embroidery around the cuffs and down the front.

Gold sandals are the traditional feminine footwear, while gold jewelry forms a major part of the complete attire. Eritrean women love jewelry. Their earrings, necklaces, rings, arm bands, and bracelets used to be made of silver or wood, but the preferred material is gold. Decorative tattoos are very popular in the villages. Many women tattoo their gums using thorns dipped in charcoal dye to make their teeth appear whiter. The traditional hairstyle is called quno (KOO-noh). Fine braids of hair stick close to the scalp and spray out from the nape like a giant fan.

Men in the countryside, especially in the hot regions, wear the djellabia (JEL-lah-bay-ah), a loose, long-sleeved robe made of white or light-colored cotton, over loose cotton trousers. They walk in leather sandals or rubber slippers. Muslim men complete the outfit with a turban. Men on the coast walk bare-chested, with a sarong, a large piece of cloth, wrapped around them from the waist down. The Beja and Rashaida nomad traders traditionally make their clothes from animal skins, but most of them now use commercially manufactured fabrics. Eritrean boys mostly wear shorts and T-shirts, while girls wear little dresses, sometimes with a scarf. People in the cities, especially in Asmara, generally wear Western-style dress—that is, shirts or T-shirts and trousers are worn by men, and skirts and blouses are worn by women. Few women wear pants. Jackets are very popular among male Asmarinos.

LIFE IN THE CITY

Homes in urban Eritrea tend to be small. There is a living room (which may double as the children's room), a bedroom, a kitchen, and a bathroom. Most houses have electricity and running water. They are usually sparsely furnished and kept clean and tidy. In recent years apartment blocks have sprung up in Asmara. With two or three bedrooms, these new living spaces are to Asmarinos the epitome of gracious living.

In many households both parents work while the children go to school. If the mother does not have a formal occupation, she keeps herself busy with church or other voluntary activities. The children are free to play outdoors after school, and they can do so safely, even at night, thanks to a low crime rate.

Friends and neighbors often meet in bars and cafés to chat and to have coffee. A favorite pastime is to stroll along the street in the early evening. Most people in the cities even prefer to walk to and from work rather than ride the buses and horse-drawn carts that run through the towns.

A classroom in Eritrea. Even though education in Eritrea is compulsory for all children between 7 and 14 years of age, many remain illiterate due to traditional lifestyles and the cost of school fees.

WORKING HOURS

According to a 1997 government regulation, all civil servants have to work about 45 hours a week. From Monday to Friday office hours are from 7:00 A.M. to 12:00 P.M., when there is a two-hour break for lunch, and then from 2:00 to 6:00 P.M. On Fridays the lunch break starts half an hour earlier, so that Muslim workers have time to go to the mosque for their weekly devotions. Some enterprises in the private sector still stick to the old system, working from 8:00 A.M. to 5:00 P.M. from Monday to Friday, and half a day on Saturday.

There are no fixed working hours in the countryside, where the time it takes shepherds and farmers to perform their tasks depends on the season and on the condition of their animals and crops.

EDUCATION

Less than 60 percent of adult Eritreans are literate, with most people attending only about five years of formal schooling. Only 66 percent of primary school—age children and 22 percent of secondary school—age youths attend school in the country. Girls in the rural areas are less likely to go to school than boys.

Children in the lower grades study in their native languages. They gradually absorb Tigrinya, Arabic, and foreign languages, especially English, as they advance to higher levels. Children in the seventh grade and above take all their subjects in English, a legacy of the British protectorate years.

The government is taking measures to improve the country's education system. One of Eritrea's Millennium Goals is to achieve universal primary education by the year 2015. Teachers are required to attend summer courses to upgrade their skills, and more schools, including boarding schools, have been built. The University of Asmara, the only university in the country, is complemented by five colleges of higher education scattered in different parts of the country. Adult education takes place in vocational training centers located in various towns.

On average, out of every 1,000 babies born in the country, an estimated 43 die within their first year of life.

HEALTH CARE

Chronic drought and decades of war have taken a toll on the health of Eritreans. Landmines from the war tear off the limbs of wandering shepherds. Malnutrition stunts the growth of children. Malaria, bilharzia, meningitis, rabies, and tetanus affect both children and adults.

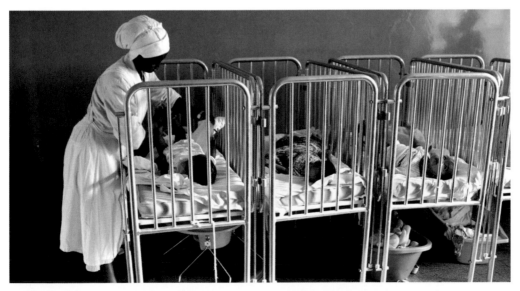

A nurse tends to the infants under her care at a hospital in Asmara. These babies are some of the more fortunate ones who have access to modern health-care facilities.

"To an Abyssinian, an hour means the whole day." Italian ethnologist Alberto Pollera made this observation in the days before the colonists brought clocks to Eritrea. However, it is still the reality today in much of rural Eritrea, where tasks are carried out in nature's time. Farmers and shepherds have no need to rush in planting crops and grazing herds. Even in the cities people go about their tasks the traditional way, according to custom. For example many of them prefer to meet in person rather than talk on the telephone. Nevertheless the Eritrean people and government are generally quite punctual in their business and office conduct.

Only 57 percent of the rural population has access to safe drinking water, and 3 percent has adequate sanitation. Residents of the cities are far more fortunate, but they still face sad conditions. Only 74 percent have access to clean drinking water, and 14 percent have access to modern sanitation facilities.

Pumps such as this one in Tessennee help to bring clean drinking water to the villagers.

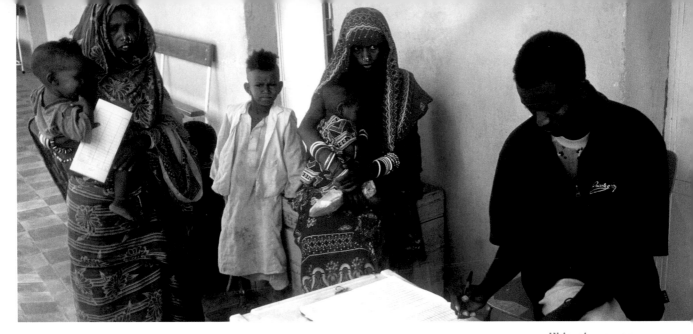

A network of clinics and small hospitals provides medical care around the country. More than 50 percent of the population lives within 3 miles (5 km) of a health facility. Asmara has two main hospitals, while seven district hospitals are located within an hour's drive from the capital. Although doctors make accurate diagnoses, they often lack the preferred medicines. The Ministry of Health is in the process of establishing a Health University in Asmara, consisting of the Orotta School of Medicine, the Asmara College of Health Sciences, and the Asmara College of Nursing and Health Technology.

Hidarab women registering for baby food at a health center in Amaleit.

SOCIAL PROBLEMS

After decades of violence, Eritreans have had enough unrest and are intent on rebuilding their country. Crime is not a serious problem. Petty theft does occur, but it is under control, because most Eritreans are ready to help catch the thief. Begging is not widespread, apart from children asking tourists for a few coins.

The main social problems are general poverty and poor living conditions, especially in the rural areas. The challenge to Eritrea is to unite efforts from the various ethnic groups to build the country's infrastructure and improve the lives of its people. With the government's stress on self-reliance and Eritreans' work ethic and nationalistic fervor, this is a challenge that the country seems ready to take.

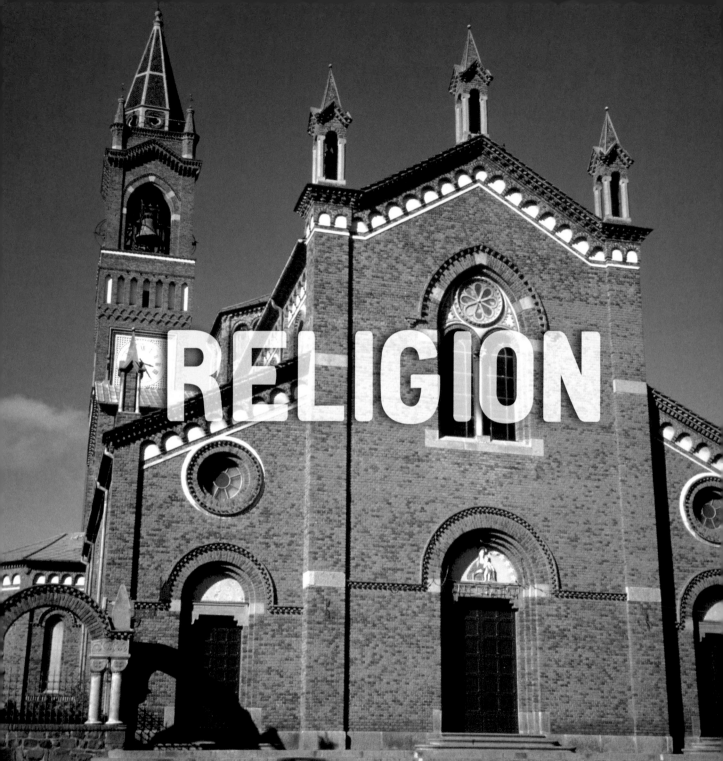

RELIGION

Women walking along the Saint Joseph's Cathedral in Asmara.
This large Romanesque style cathedral in the center of the
city was built when Eritrea was an Italian colony.

ERITREANS ARE ALMOST EQUALLY divided between Islam and Christianity. The Muslims are mainly pastoralists who live in the western plain and along the coast, while the Christians are largely Tigrinya peasants inhabiting the highlands. Islam entered Eritrea from Saudi Arabia across the Red Sea.

Geographically Islam predominates in the eastern and western lowlands, while Christianity is dominant in the highlands.

The three main faiths in Eritrea coexist in Asmara. The towers of the Catholic cathedral and the Khulafa el-Rashidin mosque stand behind the Enda Mariam Orthodox Church.

The 500-year-old Sheikh Hanafi Mosque on Massawa Island is Eritrea's oldest mosque. The walls of the courtyard are decorated with stuccowork and inside hangs a remarkable chandelier from the glassworks of Murano near Venice in Italy.

The first converts were Eritreans living on the coast; the religion then spread through the lowlands. Christianity was introduced to the coastal areas in the fourth century and later spread to the plateau. Christians in Eritrea today belong to either the Eritrean Orthodox Church or the Roman Catholic Church. There is also a small number of Protestants. Many of the smaller tribes retain their African animistic beliefs.

Although freedom of religion is ratified in the constitution, a government decree of May 2002 sanctions only four religions in Eritrea: Islam, Roman Catholicism, the Orthodox Church, and the Evangelical Church of Eritrea. All other religious groups have to be registered. Dissidents claim that registration is a tool for the government to persecute those who do not belong to the official religions.

ISLAM

Eritrean Muslims belong to the Sunni branch of Islam. Those who live in the towns go to the mosque to worship every Friday. The small Khulafa el-Rashidin mosque in Asmara, built in 1937, overflows with devotees, who spill into the street and kneel on their prayer mats, oblivious to the city traffic. The lower part of the mosque's minaret is a fluted Roman column, which hints at the country's colonial past.

Religious observance is much more diluted in the rural areas. The mosques in Muslim villages do not look much different from the huts. Although most rural Muslims dress in the Arabic style, only Rashaida women cover their faces.

Apart from the Afar, most Muslims in Eritrea do not spend much time studying the Koran, the Islamic holy book. They practice a folk version of the faith, following only some Islamic observances and retaining their pagan beliefs and customs. Most of them do not consume pork, but the same abstinence does not apply to liquor, which is also prohibited in Islam. Some ethnic groups practice polygamy, which Islam allows.

Muslims are well represented in all the towns in Eritrea, where they have made their mark in trade. The roots of their religion lie in some Dahlak Islanders, who converted to the faith in the 8th century. By the early 10th century, Massawa too had Muslim residents. However, it was not until the 16th century that Islam moved farther inland. Two factors contributed to this spread: the expansion of the Turkish Ottoman Empire into Eritrea and the forced conversions of thousands of Christians by Ahmed Gragn, the sultan of Harar. Although Islam never displaced Christianity from the highlands, it continues to dominate the lowlands of Eritrea.

Muslims praying at a mosque in Asmara.

ORTHODOX CHRISTIANITY

The **Debre Bizen** is the best-known monastery of the Eritrean Orthodox Church. Located at the top of Debre Bizen, the mountain near the town of Nefasit, the monastery contains many important Ge'ez manuscripts.

The Eritrean Orthodox Church derives from the Ethiopian Orthodox Church. Once part of the Ethiopian Orthodox Church, the Eritreans established their own branch in the 1990s that is closely tied to the church in Egypt. More than 80 percent of Christians in Eritrea belong to the Orthodox Church. Eritrean Orthodox Christianity has its origins in the Syrian Orthodox religion of the fourth century. It displays some Jewish influences in the celebration of certain festivals, such as Meskel and Kidus Yohannes. Orthodox Christians in rural Eritrea also observe the Sabbath, the rest day for Jews from Friday night to Saturday night. However, the slaughtering of animals during religious holidays is a remnant of paganism.

The Orthodox Church is very well established in Eritrea, and church activities form a significant part of daily Christian life. A prominent icon in the Orthodox Church is the Ark of the Covenant, which contains God's Ten Commandments, according to the Bible. Although some Orthodox Churches discourages reading the Bible, its followers accept the Bible as true, while also reading a few other books that are unique to their tradition. During festivals, such as Easter and Christmas, Eritrean Orthodox priests wear colorful and ornate robes and lead processions of devotees through the streets. Services are conducted in Ge'ez, the ancient language of the Aksumite Kingdom.

Because the language is no longer used today, most priests are not conversant in it. Thus they often just memorize their parts of the service. Emotions run high during church services. Devotees embrace the walls of the church and kiss the ground.

Orthodox churches are usually built on a hill. The Debre Bizen monastery sits on a plateau at 8,041 feet (2,450 m). It was founded by Abuna Filipos, who began his monastic life in 1361. The monastery survived Somali and Ethiopian invasions and holds 1,000 manuscripts in Ge'ez. The most important building for Eritrean Orthodox Christians is the Enda Mariam Church in Asmara. Built in 1917 it combines Italian and Ethiopian religious styles. Its twin towers are a useful landmark, and its interior is adorned with interesting murals.

The Eritrean and Ethiopian Orthodox Churches have their own calendar. Each month has 30 days, and the extra days left at the end of the year make up a short 13th month. This calendar was used during the Ethiopian occupation of Eritrea. Since independence, however, the Eritrean government replaced it with the Gregorian calendar used by most of the rest of the world.

Enda Mariam, Asmara's Orthodox Cathedral, is dedicated to Saint Mary. Above the wooden doors there is a colorful mosaic piece depicting religious scenes done by the Italian painter Nenne Sanguineti Poggi in the 1950s.

ROMAN CATHOLICISM

A latecomer in Eritrea, Roman Catholicism draws its followers from the Tigrinya and Kunama ethnic groups. The Roman Catholic Church has also attracted more converts in the towns, with its promise of higher education. The first Roman Catholic missionaries were Portuguese priests, who arrived in the 16th century. Their interest in Eritrea was political as much as religious. While trying to convert the population, they also helped the Abyssinians fight the invading Turks.

It was also through a missionary that Italy managed to get a foothold in Eritrea. One of the first Italians in the country was Father Giuseppe Sapeto, who established a mission in Adua and helped the Italian government purchase land in Eritrea. With the setting up of the Italian colony in 1890, more Eritreans became Catholics.

Catholics in Eritrea are very devout and devote much time to church activities. Services are held weekly on Saturday and Sunday, and it is the same for the Eritrean Orthodox Church. Conducted in Italian or Latin as well as in local languages, services are joyful occasions, full of song and praise.

The Catholic Cathedral on Liberation Avenue in Asmara was built by Italian architect Scanavini in 1922. It provides a beautiful view of the city from the top. Atop the cupola is a statue of an angel cast in bronze.

In contrast with Muslim graves, which are much simpler in design, Catholic and Orthodox graves are richly decorated with crosses and other sculptures. Catholic homes typically display a large amount of religious imagery, such as crucifixes and pictures of saints.

The interiors of a Catholic church in Asmara.

TRADITIONAL BELIEFS

Many Eritreans believe that evil spirits can take animal form to plague human beings with sickness and accidents. For example the Tigre fear the evil spirit Zar, which they believe possesses people, sometimes driving them to

RELIGIOUS OBSERVANCES

The weekly worship day for Christians is Sunday. One day in every month is also devoted to commemorating a saint or legendary king. They believe that these monthly observances purge their sins, thereby easing their access to paradise. The most common of these holidays are Michael, Gabriel, Medhanie Alem, and Be'ale Egziabiher. On these days believers go to an early morning service, and then rest the day away, abstaining even from housework.

The saint's day is sometimes celebrated with a pilgrimage. The most colorful of these is the Mariam De'arit pilgrimage near Keren. Every year on May 21 Catholics flock to the town from all over the country to pray for miracles. A small shrine is set in a baobab tree some distance from the town. After the early morning service, cows and oxen are slaughtered, and a big feast takes place, lasting late into the afternoon.

Muslims also perform pilgrimages in honor of the descendants of the Prophet Muhammad, although most of them are too poor to go to the holy city, Mecca. The most famous Muslim pilgrimage in Eritrea takes place in Keren. Believers first join in a feast of rice, cooked meat, coffee, and tea. Prayers are then said, after which the solemn atmosphere breaks into lively games and dancing. At the end of the day, money is collected for the relatives of the Prophet.

their deaths. Only a shaman can enter into a trance and communicate with the spirits to exorcise demons and cure diseases. To protect themselves from spirits, believers in animism wear amulets, which sometimes contain verses of the Koran.

The various ethnic groups also have their own slants on animism. To the Afar, for example, trees and groves as well as the dead have special powers, and they hold an annual "feast of the dead" to appease the spirits of the dead. The Beja believe that some people have the power to curse others by giving them the "evil eye." The Nara and Kunama believe in a supernatural being in heaven called Ana, whom they pray to for blessings on their harvests.

Believers in animism also perceive droughts as a punishment for their sins. As such, they engage in rain-making rituals and slaughter livestock in the hope that their sacrifices will earn them forgiveness.

Although animism is the indigenous belief system in Eritrea, some of its rituals, such as animal sacrifices, have also found their way into the local practice of "imported" faiths.

LANGUAGE

An Eritrean reading a newspaper in Asmara.

ERITREANS SPEAK A NUMBER OF languages depending on their ethnic and social backgrounds. Linguists have identified nine indigenous languages in Eritrea.

There is no national language, but the working languages are Tigrinya, spoken by the Tigrinya ethnic group, and Arabic, spoken by the Muslim section of the population. The minority groups have their own languages and dialects, and many of their members speak Tigrinya or Arabic as well.

English is the language of instruction in secondary schools and the University of Asmara. It is fast becoming the foreign language of choice for Eritreans.

Eritreans having a friendly chat. The older generation, particularly in Asmara, still speaks Italian inherited from their colonial past.

Eritreans are proud of their indigenous languages. During the years of the Ethiopian occupation, Amharic, the language of Ethiopia, was made the official language, and Eritrean languages were banned. But most Eritreans refused to speak Amharic. Instead, they continued to teach their native language to their children. Their attachment to Tigrinya became a political statement of their resistance to the occupation.

TIGRINYA

Tigrinya is a descendant of Ge'ez, an ancient language that is now used only in the Eritrean Orthodox Church. Tigrinya is a guttural language that may sound quite gruff and harsh to those hearing it for the first time. Many Tigrinya words are pronounced at the back of the throat.

For the newcomer Tigrinya is not just difficult to speak but difficult to learn as well. This is because it has many grammatical rules and there are few helpful dictionaries. Tigrinya has its own script of more than 200 characters, each representing a different sound. The consonants, such as "g" and "k," are usually hard, and "r" is always slightly rolled on the tongue. The combination "ts" is sounded on the tip of the tongue as in the English word *pits*. The vowels are pronounced either short or long. The letter "a," for example, is long as in the English word *hard* while the letter "e" is short as in the English word *bed*.

A signboard outside the Volvo restaurant in Massawa reads "Restaurant & Bar" in Tigrinya, Arabic, and English.

Tigrinya was spoken and written possibly as early as the 13th century. However, the oldest available text is the Code of Logo Sarda from the 19th century. The language made considerable progress with the sociolinguistic work of European settlers in Eritrea and is now spoken by nearly half the population—specifically the half that is of Tigrinya ethnicity.

A related language is Tigre, which is believed to be a direct descendant of Ge'ez. However, the two languages are not mutually intelligible. Tigre uses the same script as Tigrinya but varies in pronunciation and usage, depending on the geographical origin of the speaker.

A young pupil studies Arabic at an Islamic school in Keren.

ARABIC

Arabic is another Semitic language spoken by a significant proportion of Eritreans. It is the native language of the Rashaida tribe, and many Tigre speak Arabic in addition to their native tongue. The Muslim portion of the population needs to know the language in order to read the Koran. Furthermore the use of Arabic is spreading in the country, as refugees continue to return from Sudan and the Middle East, bringing with them their mastery of the language. Like Tigrinya, Arabic is full of guttural tones and sounds made in the back of the throat. The language contains three short and three long vowels. Words always start with a single consonant followed by a vowel. The Arabic script, consisting of 17 characters, is written from right to left. The addition of dots above and below the characters produces a total of 28 letters in the Arabic alphabet.

COMMON COURTESIES

Eritreans are a hospitable people. They often approach foreigners in the street to ask where they are from and how they like Eritrea.

The expected greeting at formal meetings is to shake hands with each person, asking about his or her health and family. In the more casual circumstances, Eritreans wish one another *selam* (peace). Close friends of the same gender kiss each other on both cheeks. Former fighters, however, have the most unique greeting style: They clasp their right hands together and bump their shoulders three times. In Arabic-speaking regions friends who have not seen one another for a while greet by touching right cheeks, then left cheeks, and right cheeks again.

Eritreans rarely thank others for little favors. This is perhaps because the literal translation of "thank you," *yekeniely* (YUH-ke-nee-lih) in Tigrinya, sounds too solemn for everyday situations. Besides, Eritreans do not expect thanks for the small favors they do for others. Most of them take mutual help among friends and acquaintances for granted.

Friends freely help one another, expecting no thanks in return.

MINORITY LANGUAGES

Each ethnic group in Eritrea has its own language. Apart from Arabic, Tigrinya, and Tigre, all other languages in Eritrea are spoken, substituting the lack of their own script with Latin or Arabic script. These minority languages belong to two main groups—the Cushitic and Nilotic—but they may share no similarities, even within their individual language group. Furthermore each language may have several dialect variations.

An illustration of a king on horseback beside a tethered dragon is pictured in a Bible written in Ge'ez, an ancient Ethiopic script.

Afar, Beja, Bilen, and Saho are Cushitic languages. Afar and Saho are closely related. Beja is considered one of the oldest languages in the Cushitic group. It is interesting to note that in the Beja language, the word *Tigre* means "slave." For the Beja people the Tigre language itself is associated with being a servant. Bilen, spoken mainly in and around Keren, uses Ge'ez script.

Believed to be among the earliest languages in Eritrea, Kunama and Nara belong to the Nilotic group. Although both use Latin script, the two languages are mutually unintelligible, and Nara speakers speak Tigre or Arabic to communicate with the Kunama. There is considerable dialect variation within Nara. Although some languages spoken in Sudan are related to Nara, Kunama has no known related language. There are some who consider Ilit, spoken in a region in the western lowlands, to be a relative, but others describe Ilit as a Kunama dialect. Barka is the main Kunama dialect and is understood by all Kunama Eritreans.

Most minority language speakers are bilingual, especially those who have attended high school. Bilen youth, for example, mix their speech with Arabic. In general Bilen Christians speak Tigrinya in addition to their native language, while the Muslims speak Tigre or Arabic. Within their community, for example, 60 percent of the Christians are bilingual in Tigrinya, and 70 percent of the Muslims are bilingual in Tigre.

FOREIGN INFLUENCES

The most lasting foreign influence on Eritrean languages is Italian. Many older Asmarinos use Italian in their everyday conversations with friends of the same age. Eritreans in general pepper their conversations with Italian words. Shop signs in Asmara and other big cities sport Italian names. However it is in food-related industries that the use of Italian words is most pronounced, as Eritreans have adopted the Italian names for foods that do not feature in their traditional menu. This is done sometimes wholesale and sometimes with slight modifications. For example, "cheese" and "carrots" are *formaggio* and *carote*, exactly as in Italian, but tomatoes are *pommidere*, not *pomidoro*.

More and more English words are making their way into Eritrean speech today, especially in the fields of business and technology. The use of English will become more widespread in the country, as more children learn the language in school, and as the country progresses and opens up to the rest of the world.

An increasing number of Eritrean children learn English in school. The use of English will grow as the urban world of business and technology gradually spreads through this developing nation.

MASS MEDIA

The Eritrean government exercises strict control over the media in the country. Dissension is not tolerated, and the media are expected to project the government in a good light. According to Reporters Without Borders, Eritrea is the country with the least press freedom in the world.

In 2001 the government shut down the private press and a few months later detained several journalists. Today the Ministry of Information publishes one newspaper each in Tigrinya, Arabic, and English. The *Tigrinya Hadas Eritrea* reaches a circulation of 60,000, while the Arabic *Eritrea Alhadisa* puts out more than 5,000 copies daily. The twice-weekly *Eritrea Profile* is the only English newspaper. Not only does it contain news reports and cultural analyses, but it also serves as a mouthpiece for the government. Its electronic version is available on the Internet for the benefit of the diaspora. Many online papers are critical of the Eritrean government.

The country has a government-owned television station broadcasting on two channels and two radio stations that emit on three channels. Television broadcasts cover the whole country, but very few people in the rural areas have access to a television set. Eritreans living in the cities get to watch bulletins from international agencies such as CNN and BBC, but only after they have been reviewed by the government. Radio reaches most of the rural population and is the best way to disseminate information and promote education.

An Internet café in Massawa.

The Fiat Tagliero in Asmara is one of the most famous examples of Italian Art Deco architecture in Eritrea. A former gas station, it was built in 1938 to resemble an airplane.

E RITREA IS AN ANCIENT LAND WITH many archaeological treasures. Rock paintings, pottery, and calligraphy from the times of the country's early inhabitants provide the present generation with clues to their ancestry.

Right after independence, the Eritrean population focused its attention on building the economy, and progress in the arts was minimal. The little artistic expression that surfaced during Ethiopian rule was limited to nationalistic images of fighters and patriotic songs of protest. Many artists in the country still draw inspiration from their struggle for freedom and still define themselves as witnesses of the liberation war.

A guide points out the abundant and well-preserved prehistoric paintings near Senafe in Eritrea.

The Raimoc Awards are presented to individuals and groups who most excel at literature, music, painting, drama, and traditional folklore.

Women selling handcrafted black pots at a market in Eritrea.

Nevertheless the collection of diverse cultures in this new nation has sustained the existence of a colorful tapestry of traditional handicrafts, music, dance, paintings, and poems. The various foreign influences since the time of the Turkish invasion have also left their artistic imprint on the architecture of the old buildings that still stand in the main towns. The colonial era, in particular, saw a blooming of the arts, with a distinct penchant for Italian styles. Asmara itself looks like an open-air Art Deco museum with its beautiful buildings and monuments.

As Eritrea develops economically, local artists are finding more room and opportunity to express themselves, not only to their fellow citizens, but also to the world at large. An Art Lovers Club in Asmara brings together highly creative people who meet to showcase their talents and learn from one another. Art exhibitions are also staged on a regular basis in the capital as well as in Massawa.

PAINTING

Most contemporary paintings before 1983 portrayed the ubiquitous EPLF flag or the body of a dead soldier. They were a very effective medium of propaganda in uplifting the spirits of the people, but they did little to advance the cause of art. Eritrean artists did not start exploring their cultural heritage and local landscapes in their creations until President Afwerki exhorted them to diversify their subject matter.

Most Eritrean artists have never received formal training beyond, perhaps, a few workshops under the tutelage of the EPLF army's single professional artist during the liberation years. Consequently, their straight-from-the-heart art combines raw, primitive talent with real, spontaneous emotion. During the war painters coped with the scarcity of art materials by blending their own paints from leaves and using sacks of wheat flour covered in milk powder as canvases.

The Sawa National Service Camp contributes to artistic development among young men and women by providing them with supplies and lessons. Many budding artists only discover their talent when they touch paintbrush to canvas, and some acquire enough artistic skill to eventually take on painting as a career. The EPLF art program has produced several professional painters, one of whom is Eduardo Araia, whose creations usually display a political sensitivity. Michael Adonai, another alumnus of the EPLF Cultural establishment, has won several art competitions, including the Raimoc Award.

Painted murals of freedom fighters from the war of independence with Ethiopia still stand in the streets of Asmara.

A mural in an Eritrean Orthodox monastery.

Habtom Mehret'ab is a prominent Eritrean cartoonist, who started drawing at age 11. He is also a painter, using people and landscapes as his subjects, and teaches art at the Asmara Model School. Although his earlier cartoons contained political messages, his current ones portray the lighter side of life. They have appeared in several local publications.

Another store of paintings in Eritrea consists of the colorful murals that adorn the walls of the Eritrean Orthodox churches and monasteries.

LITERATURE

The most prominent book in a local language is *Kl'e Mensa*, written in 1913 by Karl Gustav Roden, a Swede.

Eritrean literature is still in its infancy owing to the general absence of a literary heritage. Folk tales and legends have been passed down largely through oral tradition. Although the country has its store of scholarly writings, those from before the 20th century are in Ge'ez, a dead language that only Orthodox Christian Eritreans still come into contact with when attending church services. Books sold in stores are mainly in Tigrinya and Arabic, while books in English are available at the British Council Library and in stores in Asmara.

Negusse Elfu is a legendary hero whose exploits are recounted in many poems among the Tigrinya people. The poems lament his death, and minstrels sing them in a sorrowful manner to the accompaniment of the local guitar and violin. Negusse was a rebel who left his native village to serve a foreign lord, rose in rank and power, and then returned to rule his native village. He died in his prime, by the hand of a traitor. Negusse's heroic deed was killing a lion. His destiny is captured in this folk ballad:

"O Negusse, Negusse son of Elfu,
Didn't you wield a two-edged sword, and fire a two-barreled gun?
Yes, you were mightier than the mighty
Oh Negusse, the pupil of my eye . . .

"O how large must have been their number, and how much evil their intentions
To have been able to overpower you, and to have slain you at last?
Now look what our people have done.
Yes, look what the fools have done.
When they could have tilled the land and traveled on it in quiet and calm
When they could have made themselves rich and gathered honey to brew their mead

"They chose instead to destroy their own fortress.
Whose fortress did they think they have destroyed
But their own mighty fortress and with it their pride.
Oh, Negusse see how vain is this world of mortals
See how they like to make fun, carrying your leather garment and sandals
To the village market along with your gun, where merchants bargain over your gown
Your blood-stained sword making news in town.
Alas, they think they could make a profit of sale
Nay, they only broke our own hearts, causing us to weep and wail."

The first novel written in Tigrinya was *A Story of a Conscript* by Ghebreyesus Hailu. Written in 1927, but published in 1949, it tells the story of a group of Eritreans forced to fight for the Italians in Libya. Other novels that followed were also based on the same themes of opposition to colonialism and family relationships.

Independent Eritrea is nurturing many native authors, who write in their native tongues. Writers and poets are producing increasing amounts of poetry, fiction, and drama. One of the best known is Alemseged Tesfay, a lawyer turned historian-cum-novelist who fought in the war against Ethiopia. Several of his plays and short stories were translated into English. A poet who writes in both Tigrinya and English is Reesom Haile. His first English language collection was *We Have Our Voice*, which was also recorded as a CD with the poet's own voice.

MUSIC, SONG, AND DANCE

The Asmara Music School had its first graduates in 1994. The school sprang from an EPLF project, which was initiated some 15 years earlier and aimed to preserve the country's musical traditions by teaching the children music.

A man beats a traditional drum to set the rhythm for ceremonial music.

Eritrean music uses a lot of percussion and string instruments. Drums are important in setting the rhythm for the melody provided by the *kirar* (KEE-rahr) or the *chira wata* (CHEE-ruh WAH-tuh), the local guitar and violin respectively. The kirar has five strings and can play only five notes. Folk music is very popular in both the urban and rural areas. A performance is always well attended, and members of the audience often show their enthusiasm and appreciation by climbing onto the stage to kiss and hug the performers. It is also common for Eritrean fans to dance and sing along with their music idols, or to stick banknotes on the foreheads or in the hands of the performers.

The first Eritrean to record Tigrinya songs on a compact disc was Abraham Afewerki. He was popular because his songs were evocative of Eritrea's culture, and his socially conscious lyrics were very inspiring. Among his contributions to Eritrean music is his modification of the kirar to play 12 notes. The Abubakar and Stanley Band, based in the Netherlands, aims to gain international recognition for Eritrean pop music.

Eritrean dancing is mainly feet-shuffling and shoulder-jerking. It looks like a cross between African and Asian dance, accompanied by mild music with loud drumming. Every ethnic group has its own dance style, and the most beautiful dancers come from the Kunama tribe. They dance in couples, freely expressing their emotions through graceful, and sometimes suggestive, moves. Tigre and Bilen women dance the *sheleel* (SHO-leel) in groups, swinging their long plaited hair vigorously across their faces.

Rashaida women in their burqa veils dance as the men clap and sing at a wedding in Eritrea.

Colorful indigenous handicrafts are attractive items at the markets.

HANDICRAFTS

Every ethnic group in Eritrea has a handicraft specialty. The Nara tribe is famous for saddles and baskets. Young Nara girls learn how to make coiled baskets from their mothers. These baskets are customarily made from natural materials, but contemporary versions have incorporated yarn in vibrant colors. The baskets are used at weddings and other celebrations.

Men in the Beni-Amer ethnic group always carry on them a cross-shaped dagger, which they make themselves. A curved, two-edged blade and a big ebony hilt give the dagger a distinctive shape, which displays a strong Arabic influence.

Jewelry is another traditional handicraft. Silversmiths in the region around Keren create beautiful ornaments, which they sell in the market. Eritrean women of all ethnicities are very fond of silver and gold necklaces, bracelets, and belts.

This penchant for adornment that many ethnic groups in the country share extends to adding color wherever possible. Color is a defining characteristic of many indigenous handicrafts. Besides baskets, mats, and injera tray covers, even the clothes that the Eritreans wear display a myriad colors. Rashaida dress, in particular, is multicolored and decorated with beads. Baby carriers have shells sewn onto them.

Carvings are a traditional handicraft shared by all the ethnic groups in the country. Using basic tools and raw materials such as wood and clay, sculptors create an assortment of figures, including human and animal shapes, bowls, and trays. One of the best sculptors in Eritrea today is Kibrom Garza. He learned the art from the masters in his native village, and his works have attracted many admirers since he began as a young sculptor. His specialty is the *mido* (MEE-doh), a wooden comb traditionally worn by men in their hair. Kibrom does not sell his sculptures, and his *Massacre of Shiib* in soft wood is considered a masterpiece.

THEATER

Drama is an ancient art form in Eritrea and was traditionally staged to celebrate religious festivals. During the war for independence the EPLF performed short skits all over Eritrea to stir up local resistance against Ethiopian oppression. Today theater is growing more popular in Eritrea as a channel of artistic expression.

An intricate design in Arabic carved into the lintel on a building in Massawa.

A boy hugs a lute, one of many traditional musical instruments at the disposal of modern Eritrean theater.

In Asmara foreign classics are staged regularly in native languages at the Opera House. A production of Ibsen's *A Doll's House* running from 2009 to 2010 was performed in Tigrinya by actors from the PFDJ Cultural Group in cooperation with the Norwegian government. To bring the play closer to the Eritrean audience, the characters' names were changed to local ones, and the play carefully adapted to a contemporary Eritrean middle-class context. Conversely Alemseged Tesfay's *The Other War* has been performed in the English language in Europe and appeared in an English anthology of African plays.

Eritrea is, however, making progress in creating its own works for the stage. With a traditional foundation in dance and music, indigenous theatrical groups supported by international cultural organizations are gradually integrating native dance and music with modern dramatic skills. The various ethnic groups are also exploring their cultural heritage to write plays in their own languages.

The British Council is one foreign organization that actively contributed to the development of theater in Eritrea. In 1997 it collaborated with two other foreign bodies to run two training courses for native artists. The first course trained Tigre and Bilen artists who then devised original plays that they performed for local audiences in various parts of the country. The second project took 12 graduates from a previous course to two villages to work with Tigrinya-speaking natives in developing homegrown theater. Leeds University has also sent representatives to Eritrea to carry out research on Tigre cultural performances.

Original Eritrean theater often takes the struggle against Ethiopian domination as a major theme. For example the Eritrea Festival 2000 in Asmara showcased a musical theater performance called *Menfes Mekhete*

(Spirit of Resistance). Focused on the fight against foreign oppression, the drama opened with a scene in which Ethiopian soldiers killed Eritrean civilians. There was no dialogue; instead the play used songs in the local languages, body gestures, colorful costumes, and lighting to convey its meaning. In one scene, actors dressed in red held lighted candles on their heads to represent those who had shed their blood in the liberation war and lighted the way for future generations.

Children's theater has bloomed under the guidance of Issayas Tseggai, a war veteran devoted to the cause of advancing Eritrean arts. Started in 1994 the Sewit Children's Group brings together 20 youngsters between the ages of 10 and 16 who have undergone training in music, dance, and drama. The group prefers to tour the countryside, performing skits and short plays that relate directly to the experience of Eritrean children. They have also been commissioned by UNICEF to produce a play on landmines as part of an international project on Mine Action Education. Tseggai believes the group has now attained a standard high enough to perform on any stage in the world. He envisions them performing in Europe.

The theater on Harnet Avenue in Asmara was built by the Italians in 1919.

LEISURE

For rural Eritreans, enjoying the country's scenic
natural landscape is a simple, well-loved activity.

LIFE IS HARSH FOR THE AVERAGE Eritrean. Rural life presents few forms of leisure to choose from. Besides standard games such as hide-and-seek, children may act out adult responsibilities, such as loading the camels or doing the household chores.

. . . .

"If you prepare
coffee, something
calls people
to come."
—An Eritrean
saying

Afar children play a form of chess using camel droppings. Town life features a wider range of recreational activities, such as relaxing at a café, watching a film, and shopping. Eritreans love the outdoors, too. Cycling and soccer are the country's top sports.

A night out with friends is a popular activity among Eritreans living in the city.

The National Museum of Eritrea in Asmara. Inaugurated in 1992 by Woldeab Woldemariam, the museum presents and promotes Eritrean history to both the locals and outsiders alike.

Special centers set up by the government promote sports and culture for young people. These occupy children and teenagers with healthy recreational programs, which equip them with useful skills and knowledge at the same time. Children would otherwise play in the streets, putting themselves as well as motorists in danger. Young Asmarinos typically roam the streets at night, attracted by the neon lights in the city center.

RELAXING IN ASMARA

Asmarinos are far more fortunate than Eritreans elsewhere in the country. In addition to going to the movies and hanging out at cafés, they get to enjoy plays and exhibitions organized by the British Council or the Alliance Française. Concerts and dance performances by both homegrown and foreign groups also spice up the entertainment scene in the Eritrean capital.

The National Museum is a place of attraction for locals as well as for tourists. It showcases artifacts from the excavations of the Aksumite port, Adulis; scrolls in the ancient Ge'ez language; Italian paintings; and items from Emperor Haile Selassie's reign. The museum garden displays Italian cannons and machine guns.

CINEMA

Going to the movies used to be considered a decadent activity, associated with a life of luxury. Since independence, however, the government has stressed the importance of film as a constructive art form with educational and recreational value. Ticket prices have been kept low to make movies affordable to more Eritreans. Movie theaters in Asmara, such as the one built in 1918 along Liberation Avenue, have been renovated to offer more comfortable seating and better projection equipment. The smaller towns, however, still make do with open-air cinemas. Owning a home video player does not seem to keep Eritreans away from the movie theaters, where they can catch the latest Hollywood blockbusters and Arabic dramas. However, tight censorship mercilessly cuts out scenes that are considered politically subversive or physically revealing.

The annual Asmara Film Festival was initiated in 1996 to encourage more Eritreans to go to the movies. Staged in collaboration with foreign embassies and various cultural organizations, the festival has screened films from the United States, Europe, Africa, and the Middle East, and has succeeded in pulling in the crowds to the movie theaters.

The most important soccer tournament in Eritrea is the Eritrean Premier League. Getting an opportunity to play in this competition is a great honor for Eritrean players.

The Cinema Impero, or Cinema Empire, is an Art Deco-style cinema built by the Italians in Asmara in 1937. Forty-five round lights decorate the front of this building's façade.

This pool hall in Asmara provides numerous activities for the youth of Eritrea.

YOUTH CLUBS

Government-run youth clubs are important meeting places for young people in the cities. They organize educational as well as recreational programs, such as woodwork or metalwork for young men and sewing or home economics for young women. Debates, quizzes, and other competitions test the members' general knowledge. The most popular activity, however, is soccer. The club in Massawa has 32 soccer teams consisting of players between the ages of 8 and 14 years.

The National Union of Eritrean Youth and Students (NUEYS) is a nongovernmental organization whose objective is to work for the betterment of Eritrean youth both in the country and within the diaspora. It is mainly an educational group, with members taking part in 33 environmental conservation initiatives and health education. It conducts seminars and campaigns on youth empowerment and raises gender issues, particularly girls' education. Members also take part in recreational and sporting activities.

COFFEE

A major social activity is the coffee ceremony. The making of Eritrean coffee, called *bun* (BOON), is an elaborate affair. The preparation is always the woman's job. The hostess sets the mood by burning incense. Once everyone is seated, she sits down on a low stool and roasts the raw coffee beans in a shallow pan over a small charcoal fire. The smoking beans are passed around to the guests so that they can smell the aroma. Both the hostess and the guests use their hands to waft the smoke toward their faces.

When the house is filled with the wonderful smell of roasted coffee beans, the hostess grinds

A woman is making coffee in the traditional Eritrean fashion.

the beans in a mortar using a pestle. She then transfers the ground coffee into a round clay pot with a long neck and a tube-like spout. Some people add a little crushed ginger as well. The hostess pours water into the pot and brings the coffee slowly to a boil. Letting it boil over invites shame, so as soon as the mixture starts to boil, the hostess removes it from the fire, lets it cool slightly, and then returns the pot to the fire. She repeats this step several times to attain the desired strength.

After an hour the coffee is finally served in tiny cups with lots of sugar. Popcorn is passed around to accompany the coffee. The entire coffee-making process is repeated as many times as it takes to ensure that all the guests have had their fill. Everyone should drink at least three cups and compliment the taste. A hostess may react to the lack of compliments from her guests by pouring away the prepared coffee and brewing a fresh pot.

Cyclists stop for a rest near a café in Asmara.

CYCLING

Cycling is one of the most popular sports in the country. Cycling clubs are found everywhere, and many women also take the sport seriously.

The cycling federation organizes bike races at regional and interclub levels, as well as celebrates national holidays. During these events thousands of spectators turn out in the streets to cheer the racers on. One of the toughest races in the country takes place on the Asmara-Keren road. The 50-mile (80-km) route, which winds up and down steep slopes, tests and sharpens the skills of the best cyclists in the country. These go on to race in international competitions, such as the *Tour de France* or the *Giro d'Italia*, which Eritreans watch intently at home.

SOCCER AND OTHER SPORTS

Soccer is another national obsession, although it is male-dominated. There are more than 200 soccer clubs and more than 5,000 registered players throughout the country. Although there are no professional soccer clubs in Eritrea, some Eritreans do play professionally in foreign leagues. Registered players hold regular full-time jobs and confine their training and matches to the weekends. The national federation organizes regional league and championship games for both adults and the youth, and matches are watched by thousands of ardent fans. Despite the lack of playing fields and sports equipment, almost every Eritrean male plays soccer with gusto. Soccer fanatics also follow the games of European clubs, especially the Italian ones, and international teams. The national soccer team takes part in the African championship and other regional tournaments.

Eritrea's track team has run races and marathons in the All Africa Games. The National Union of Eritrean Women has two volleyball teams, and the Asmara Volleyball Federation regularly organizes local tournaments. A basketball contest has even been organized for disabled war veterans living in Asmara.

Wealthy Asmarinos can play tennis at the club and go horseback riding. Eritreans have many good beaches in Assab and Massawa to go for a swim in the sun. Many young people in the cities are also avid basketball players, being influenced by returnees from the United States.

Young people playing soccer in the streets of Massawa.

FESTIVALS

Colorfully robed Eritreans come together to celebrate the Meskal festival.

>HOME TO A DIVERSE POPULATION, Eritrea celebrates many festivals during the year. Most of these are religious and traditional in nature. For example the arrival of the rains and the end of the harvest are causes for celebration among the farming population.

There are also several secular national holidays, which mark significant events in the political and social history of the country, such as its independence day. An entire clan or village may also gather to celebrate milestones in the life of individual members.

An old man dances in front of the traditional bonfire at the Meskal festival celebration in Asmara.

While encouraging Eritreans to have fun, the government also advises them to reduce the wastefulness of feasting and drinking.

Eritrean Orthodox priests, holding silver and gold crosses, say the ceremonial prayers during the the colorful Timkat festival, which marks the Epiphany of Christ.

The Aba Samuel song goes like this: "Samuel, Samuel, give us something for Michael's sake. I trusted Samuel and descended the ravine where only lions dare."

The main ingredients for a complete festival are food, drink, music, and dance. Prayers and spiritual rituals form the focus of many celebrations, as religion plays an important role in Eritreans' daily life. Finally feasting with relatives and friends tops off the holiday. Christian festivals are generally full of pomp, while Muslim celebrations tend to be more muted.

CHRISTIAN HOLIDAYS

On festival day Orthodox Christians in Eritrea go to church in their best clothes. After the service the priests lead the congregation in a street procession, and the rest of the day is spent feasting and having fun. The priests are always served the best food and wine at these feasts.

Timket, which falls on January 19, is the most important festival for Orthodox Christians in Eritrea. It commemorates the baptism of Jesus in the Jordan River. On Timket Eve people flock outdoors in lively and colorful processions. Then on the day itself the priests parade a small cloth-covered chest, symbolizing the Ark of the Covenant, through the streets. The congregation follows them to a pool or river to witness the reenactment of Jesus's baptism. They celebrate with a feast after the parade.

HOLIDAYS IN ERITREA

The Eritrean government has declared 17 public holidays per year. This number may seem large, but it is the only way to ensure that the various religious groups in the country are well represented.

The National Holidays	The Fixed Christian Holidays
January 1: New Year's Day	*January 7: Genna (Orthodox Christmas)*
March 8: International Women's Day	*January 19: Timket (Orthodox Epiphany)*
May 1: Labor Day	*September 11: Enkutatash (Orthodox New Year)*
May 24: Liberation Day	*September 27: Meskel (Finding of the true cross)*
June 20: Martyrs' Day	*December 25: Christmas*
September 1: National Day	
December 8: Children's Day	

The dates for Fasika (Orthodox Easter) and Good Friday (Orthodox) vary each year, because they follow the lunar, rather than the solar, calendar. They are always celebrated in the spring. Muslim holidays also follow the lunar calendar. Id al-Fitr (the end of the fasting month) takes place in the spring, while Id al-Hajj (the pilgrimage to Mecca) and Mawlid al-Nabi (the birthday of the Prophet Muhammad) occur in the summer.

The festival of Meskel commemorates the finding of Jesus's cross by Empress Helena (the mother of Constantine the Great) about 1,600 years ago. On September 27 devotees plant a tree in the town square and later bring tall branches or poles with yellow daisies tied at the top to this location. After the church service the priests lead the congregation to the bundle of branches in the square and set fire to it. Then everyone dances around the bonfire in celebration and sings songs.

The Kunama call the holiday of the cross *Mashkela*. Kunama villagers carry lit torches in procession to a clearing outside the village. Here they pile their torches in a huge bonfire and dance around it until the last ember flickers out. This is when they gather the new harvest and prepare a drink

from the fresh grain to offer their ancestors. Only after all these rituals have been performed do they eat of their harvest.

Catholic and Protestant Eritreans pay the most attention to Christmas. On December 25 they attend services at church, and then go home to feast and exchange presents among family and friends. Those who can afford it put up a Christmas tree and perhaps a nativity scene.

Drummers participate in the Meskel festival in Asmara. Thousands gather annually to celebrate the finding of Christ's cross by Saint Helen some 1,600 years ago.

During the feast of Sidi Bekri, pilgrims dance in a circle, taking turns to step inside, where a man waits holding a cudgel. If a volunteer can endure the flogging without flinching, he takes over the cudgel, and a new round begins.

ISLAMIC HOLIDAYS

The three most important celebrations for Muslim Eritreans are Id al-Fitr, Id al-Hajj, and Mawlid al-Nabi. Festivities for the first two can last up to 10 days in certain regions.

Id al-Fitr celebrates the end of Ramadan, the Muslim fasting month. For 30 days all Muslims, except for the very young, the very old, and the infirm, eat or drink nothing from sunrise to sunset. This is a time given to prayer, meditation, and introspection. On the morning of Id al-Fitr, everyone puts on new clothes, children ask their elders for forgiveness, and the men go to the mosque for special prayers. When they come back, it is time to feast with relatives and friends. Some villages organize communal games and activities. The Beni-Amer take part in camel races and competitions showcasing their swordsmanship and horsemanship.

Id al-Hajj falls on the 10th day of the 10th month of the lunar year. It celebrates the pilgrimage to the holy city of Mecca, a pilgrimage that every Muslim endeavors to fulfill at least once during his or her lifetime. On this day Muslims believe that the gates of heaven remain open for the faithful. Those who get blessings from their parents on this day are also blessed by God (or Allah). Animal sacrifices characterize this festival. Muslims slaughter sheep and offer the skins at the mosques. All families make it a point to visit their relatives on Id al-Hajj.

Mawlid al-Nabi commemorates the birth of the Prophet Muhammad. Although it is celebrated with as much fervor as Id al-Fitr and Id al-Hajj, this is usually a solemn occasion. After morning prayers all male believers gather together to enjoy cooked meat and dates with tea and coffee. The women stay at home to share a modest banquet. During Mawlid al-Nabi, Muslims recite a text entitled *Mawlid al-Nabi*, which describes the birth of the Prophet. They accompany their chanting with a dance.

NATIONAL HOLIDAYS

Eritreans devote three days each year to celebrate their nationhood. National Day falls on September 1, the day the armed struggle against the Ethiopian military regime was launched in 1961. Liberation Day, on May 24, commemorates the joyous occasion when the EPLF troops evicted the Ethiopian army from Asmara. Martyrs' Day, on June 20, remembers those who lost their lives in the fight for their country's freedom.

Women from the Tigre ethnic group perform a traditional dance at a festival in Asmara.

   The program for these events contains speeches by the president and other leaders, public demonstrations, cultural shows, sports contests, seminars, and exhibitions. At the start of official celebrations, a group of religious leaders representing the major faiths says a prayer for the country and gives their blessings to the people. Public displays aim to reinforce Eritrean patriotism and to emphasize the need to be committed to rebuilding the country. As they celebrate their hard-won freedom, Eritreans are also reminded of the difficulties that lie ahead and of the contributions that each of them has to make.

YOUTH FESTIVALS

Most festivals for children in Eritrea are religious in nature. Hiyo falls on the day after Christmas and commemorates the killing of infants by King Herod as related in the Bible. On Hiyo children visit villagers' homes and sing for a treat of roasted chickpeas. For Aba Abraham on August 27, children parade through the streets with lighted torches. When they go home, their elders walk over the torches placed on the floor and pray for a bountiful harvest.

Hoye, celebrated with burning torches, singing, and processions, takes place twice a year, on New Year's Eve and Meskel's Eve.

The festival of Aba Samuel spans two weeks in December. During this time girls go singing from house to house, and receive food and money in return. They use part of the money to buy food, which they offer to the church. They spend the rest of the money on food for themselves, and usually everyone else joins in the feast.

FAMILY CELEBRATIONS

Every milestone in the lifetime of the average Eritrean is celebrated according to Christian or Islamic traditions. Accompanied by singing, dancing, and merrymaking, celebrations usually last several days.

For babies born in a Christian family, the first life event is baptism and name-giving. Baby boys are baptized at the age of 40 days, while baby girls are baptized when they are 80 days old. Early in the morning the mother dresses herself and her baby in their best clothes and goes to church together with the baby's godparents and some relatives. The baby is baptized and named following the church service, and then everyone shares some bread. At home the parents throw a lunch party, inviting friends, neighbors, and the priest who performed the baptism. The guests bring sugar and bread for the baby.

In Muslim households circumcision is the most important childhood event, done usually at the age of seven. Girls are also circumcised despite the risk of severe injury if the operation is not done properly and under sanitary conditions. Circumcision of boys, however, is given more importance. Goats are slaughtered, relatives and friends come over with gifts, and much feasting takes place. In the evening the religious leaders arrive to do the operation, and the family offers them food, sweet syrup, and coffee. When girls are circumcised only a few guests are invited, and only porridge is eaten. In some communities the women even perform the ritual in secret.

Weddings usually take place in January, outside the harvest seasons and fasting periods. In the villages betrothals and arranged marriages are still the

THE DADDA

The Nara of the western lowlands welcome the arrival of the rains in the winter with a five-day celebration. This celebration, called the dadda, *is a form of prayer in the hope that the community will receive a bountiful harvest.*

During the dadda young men from two neighboring villages gather to perform a ritual fight. At the start of the rainy season, every young man makes two shields—one from the bark of a tree and the other from the hide of a giraffe. He also makes a stick from a special tree, and his girlfriend decorates his animal skin shield with beads. In the meantime two elders from each village go up a hill, where they kill a goat, mix its blood with some medicinal herbs, and spray the mixture all around. The ground then becomes sacred, and no human or animal is allowed on it for the next five days.

After five days the dadda begins. Accompanied by beating drums and dancing, the elders lead the young men up the hill. Dressed in only a short skirt, with their hair smothered in ointment, each young man carries his shields up the hill. Before the fight he gives the decorated shield to his girlfriend and takes up his stick and the other shield. At a signal from the elders, the young men begin the fight. They fight for an hour until the elders order them to stop. Then everybody goes back to their village, and the fighting resumes in the same manner the next day.

On the third day the fighters meet near a big stream, where they shake hands and enjoy a big feast of barbecued goat prepared by the villagers. Then they go home, put on their best clothes, and dance the night away with the rest of the village. The next day, the warriors go into the forest and hunt rabbits. Then they bring the rabbits to the middle of the village and have yet another feast. On the last day, all the villagers gather with their cattle, bringing along some milk and loaves of bread. They pour the milk over the bread and plunge into the final feast of the festival before taking their cattle to the pastures. The dadda is now complete.

norm, and families sometimes look for their children's life partners within their own clan. The bride's family pays a dowry, and the groom's family pays a bride price of cattle, jewels, and dresses. While Christians marry in church, Muslims marry at home, with the sheik officiating. In Asmara wedding parties on hotel rooftops last late into the night.

FOOD

A man dips into the food served at a restaurant in Asmara.

CHAPTER 13

ERITREAN CUISINE IS AS varied as Eritrea's people. Not only do the different ethnic groups living in the different parts of the country have unique food specialties, but they also prepare different versions of the same dishes.

However, Eritrea does not produce enough food to feed its entire population. Due to chronic drought families living in the rural areas stare famine in the face each day of their lives, wondering when they will see their next meal and where it will come from. The majority of Eritreans depend on food aid from the international community, surviving on porridge made from ground grain, flour, and water. When they have nothing to eat, the poor fill their stomachs with anything barely edible, such as wild vegetables and prickly pears. People in the urban areas, in contrast, have access to a variety of foodstuffs. For example, the Asmarino diet features Western items such as spaghetti and steak.

A grocery store in Eritrea.

In Eritrea children and mothers with newborns are given the best nutrition. This includes meat and dairy products. Children in the cities also consume mashed potatoes, fruit, and honey.

DAILY BREAD

A woman prepares injera for a meal.

A traditional Eritrean staple food is *injera*. This is a spongy, slightly sour pancake made from fermented teff, wheat, or sorghum. At mealtime the family gathers around a large tray on which layers of injera lie topped with a variety of spicy stews and sauces. *Zigni* (ZIHG-nee) is a chicken or beef stew; *alicha* (ah-LEE-cher) is a vegetable stew; and *shiro* (SHEE-roe) is a legume puree. Each person eats the meal by breaking off a chunk of *injera* from his or her side of the stack and using the chunk to scoop up some of the topping.

Another favorite staple is *kitcha* (KIT-cher), a thin, baked, unleavened bread made from wheat or barley. In general the highlanders consume teff, wheat, and barley, while the lowlanders cook with durra and millet. More oil and butter is used in the urban areas, because those living in the rural areas cannot afford these items. Meat consumption is limited to the very wealthy in Eritrea. The poor get to taste meat stews only on festival days, when the village holds a feast. The most common meat is goat, but the coastal populations also consume a fair amount of fish. Rural Eritreans get most of their protein from milk and legumes such as lentils. The poor living in the urban areas of the country substitute meat with beef tripe, which is cheap but difficult to prepare. Their alternative to injera is *shiro*. Because this spicy porridge keeps for days, many working mothers cook a big pot during the weekend, and then reheat portions of the shiro for daily meals.

Spices play an important role in Eritrean cuisine. In fact all traditional recipes in the country require at least one type of spice, and most dishes are flavored with a combination of several. *Berbere* (bear-BEAR), a blend of numerous spices and dried chilies, goes into almost everything from shiro to zigni.

BEVERAGES

Eritreans consume water, milk, and a variety of traditional drinks. Muslims generally do not drink alcoholic beverages, sticking to coffee, tea, and other unfermented drinks. Highland Muslims have a preference for *aba'ke* (ah-BAH-kay), an unfermented drink made from a lentil-like grain. Linseed is also ground and mixed with water to make a refreshing drink.

Mead in Eritrea is a nonalcoholic honey drink. Its fermented version is *mies* (MEES). Because of the high cost of honey, it is not as popular as the other homebrew, *suwa* (SOO-wah), a beer-like drink made from hops and a fine millet-like grain. *Zebib* (ZAY-bib) is an anise-flavored liquor that Eritreans usually bring with them when visiting their friends or relatives. The Afar make a very strong alcohol, called *douma* (DOE-mah), from the sap of palm trees.

Fizzy drinks are also enjoyed by young and old in Asmara and in other towns. Besides the ubiquitous Coca-Cola Eritrean urbanites like to drink *spritzi* (SPRIT-zee), which is fizzy water flavored with fruit juice. Adults enjoy tea or espresso, always with a lot of sugar. In some areas coffee is served with ginger or black pepper as well as with sugar. Blended banana, mango, or papaya juices are also common in the major cities.

Zigni is a popular Eritrean stew dish made using chicken or beef.

TABLE MANNERS

Eritrean families eat communal-style, sharing food from a large tray placed in the middle of a low dining table. Among the Tigrinya, especially, children and adults sit at separate tables, as the former are considered to have no table manners. Before a meal one of the women of the household goes around carrying a basin of water, in which everyone washes their hands. This is because Eritreans eat with their fingers.

Various types of herbs, grains, and pulses sold at the markets in Eritrea.

Then everyone sits around the table, either on the floor or on low stools, and the head of the family says grace. Each person takes from the portion of food closest to him or her, using only the right hand. It is bad manners to lick the fingers or to let them touch the lips, and it is rude to return the leftover food to the communal tray. When dinner is over the head of the family says grace again. Then the wife covers the tray with a conical lid and takes it away, amid murmurs of blessings and praises.

THE ERITREAN KITCHEN

Cooking is done by women only, especially in the rural areas. The kitchen is a small and dark space located in a small hut away from the living quarters. Few houses have running water, and one of the most important utensils is the water pot. Girls walk for hours every day to fetch water from the communal well or tap. The stove is placed on the floor, and the cook either squats or sits on a low stool to prepare meals. Most rural kitchens are equipped with wood-burning stoves, while in the towns, people use charcoal for fuel. Only the very rich families can afford gas or electricity.

Urban cooks use aluminum pots and pans, while many rural women still use utensils made of clay or wood. However, plastic spoons and bowls are fast invading rural kitchens. The mortar and pestle—a large ceramic or stone bowl and a long pole—have disappeared completely in the towns, but can still be seen in rural kitchens. Women spend a long time each day grinding the grains for making injera or porridge.

FRESH FROM THE MARKET

Fresh produce can be obtained from the many markets in both Eritrea's rural and urban areas. Large villages and small towns in the country hold weekly markets that attract people from places as far as 5 miles (8 km) away. These people come to sell their excess subsistence crops and home-reared livestock, and to pick up food supplies. Eritrean markets have everything. Although stalls selling meat, fruits, vegetables, grain, and spices are the focus of activity, market-goers can also find furniture, kitchen utensils, clothes, jewelry, and religious artifacts being sold at stalls standing on the outskirts of the main market. Surrounding the market in Keren, for example, are tailor shops and vendors of various handicrafts. Cattle and wood are traded at the edge of the town to avoid the animals causing congestion and inconveniencing the residents.

A fruit and vegetable market in Asmara is stocked with all the freshest ingredients needed for daily cooking.

Asmarinos have the added option of patronizing the supermarkets and grocery stores. The wealthier residents can even buy fine wines and chocolates from specialty Italian-style shops.

EATING OUT

Eritreans eat out mainly at lunchtime, when it is impractical to prepare their meals. Dinner, however, is usually eaten at home, as it is much cheaper to eat in. Only wealthy families can afford to dine out regularly. In the evenings the restaurants in Asmara and Massawa are mostly filled with tourists, foreign residents, and diplomats.

Most restaurants in Eritrea serve either local or Italian food. The fare may not always be up to international standards, owing to the lack of trained cooks and high-quality ingredients. Far more popular than the restaurants in Asmara are the cafés that dot the city. Some of these open early in the morning to sell breakfast favorites, such as scrambled eggs with onions and tomatoes, called *frittata* (FRI-ta-tah), and *fool* (FOOL), a bean puree. Asmarinos love to sit at the sidewalk cafés, where they chat with their friends over coffee, watching the people and traffic go by. Many cafés are equipped with a television and video player, and this draws in large evening crowds for ice cream or after-dinner drinks.

SHIRO (LEGUME PUREE)

8 servings

1½ cups (375 ml) oil

1 cup (250 ml) red onions, chopped

1 clove garlic, chopped

2 cups (500 ml) water

1½ cups (375 ml) chickpea flour

A pinch each of cinnamon, fenugreek, coriander, fennel, and red pepper

Salt to taste

- Heat oil in a pan, and fry onions and garlic until brown.
- Add water and bring to a boil.
- Sprinkle chickpea flour a little at a time, stirring constantly to prevent lumps.
- Add salt and spices.
- Cook until the mixture is smooth and thick.
- Remove from heat. Serve hot or cold.

HEMBESHA (ERITREAN BREAD)

Makes one large round loaf

2 cups (500 ml) warm water
1 tablespoon (15 ml) active dry yeast
1 tablespoon (15 ml) sugar
½ cup (125 ml) sugar
½ tablespoon (7.5 ml) salt
1 teaspoon (5 ml) black caraway seeds
6 cups (1.5 L) unbleached all-purpose flour

- Mix the yeast in the warm water and add 1 tablespoon sugar until the mixture turns frothy, about 10 to 20 minutes.

- Add the ½ cup sugar, salt, seeds, and most of the flour and mix well. You may need to use the whole 6 cups of flour. Make a nice, soft dough and knead well until the dough is smooth and elastic.

- Place the dough in an oiled bowl, cover, and let rise in a warm place until doubled in size.

- Oil a 16-inch pizza pan. Punch down the dough, knead briefly, and roll into a large circle. Place in the pan, cover with a tea towel, and let rise again in a warm place for about 30 to 40 minutes.

- With a table knife, press down completely through the dough, making 4 lines across the diameter of the loaf, dividing it into 8 pieces. Then make lines within each wedge to produce a spider web or pinwheel design and to create 3 to 4 pieces per wedge. Finally, pinch the dough around the edge at 1-inch intervals to make a fluted design.

- Bake in an oven at 350ºF (175ºC) for approximately 20 minutes, or until golden brown on top and bottom of loaf. Cool on a wire rack.

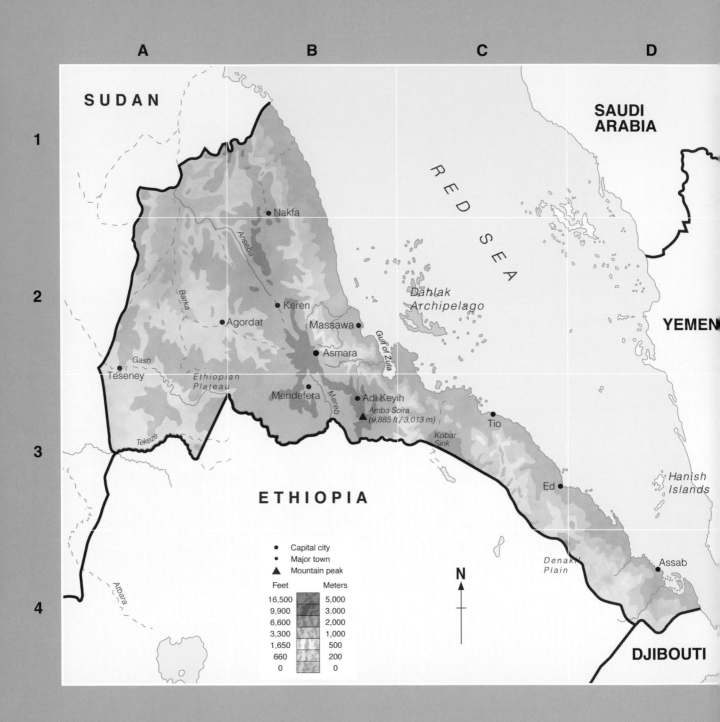

MAP OF ERITREA

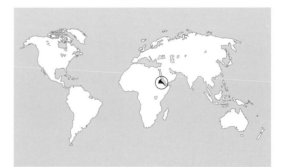

ECONOMIC ERITREA

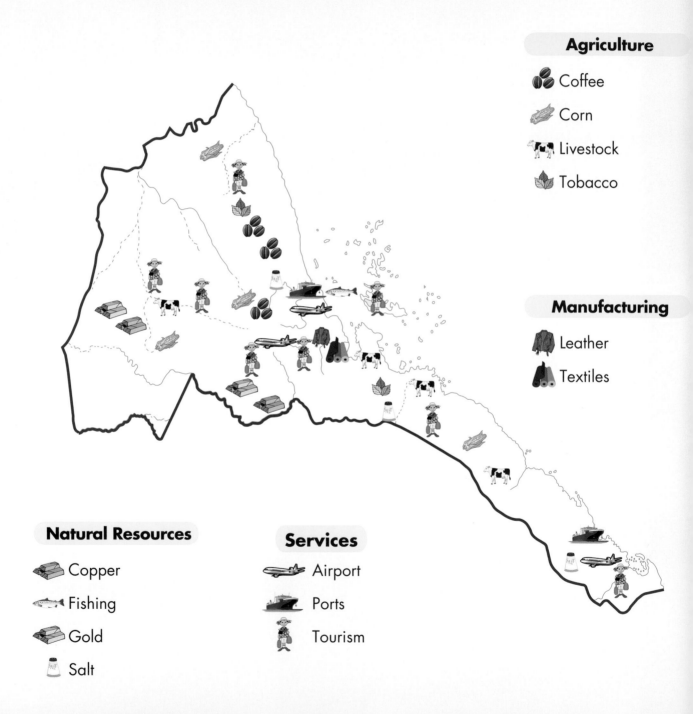

Agriculture

- Coffee
- Corn
- Livestock
- Tobacco

Manufacturing

- Leather
- Textiles

Natural Resources

- Copper
- Fishing
- Gold
- Salt

Services

- Airport
- Ports
- Tourism

ABOUT THE ECONOMY

OVERVIEW

The Eritrean economy has suffered greatly from wars and many years of drought. The restrictive economic policy practiced by the government of Isaias Afwerki keeps foreign investments away, leaving the local industry in a primitive condition. The huge army drains large amounts of resources and keeps many people out of the labor market. Eritrea is one of the poorest countries in the world and depends heavily on food aid to feed its population. At present remittances from Eritreans living abroad constitute a large share of annual GDP, and the government has placed its hopes on the mining industry to lift its economy.

GROSS DOMESTIC PRODUCT (GDP)

$3.961 billion (2009 estimate)

GDP PER CAPITA

$700 (2009 estimate)

GROWTH RATE

3.6 percent (2009 estimate)

CURRENCY

Nakfa
1 ERN=100 cents
$1=15.38 ERN (2010 estimate)

INFLATION

20 percent (2009 estimate)

LABOR FORCE

1.9 million

NATURAL RESOURCES

Gold, potash, zinc, copper, salt, oil and natural gas, fish

AGRICULTURAL PRODUCTS

Sorghum, lentils, vegetables, corn, cotton, tobacco, and sisal

INDUSTRIES

Food processing, beverages, clothing and textiles, light manufacturing, salt, cement

TOURISM

81,000 visitors (2008 estimate)

MAIN EXPORTS

Livestock, sorghum, salt, textiles, and light manufactures

MAIN IMPORTS

Processed goods, machinery, petroleum, and oil products

MAIN TRADE PARTNERS

India, Saudi Arabia, Italy, China, and Sudan

CULTURAL ERITREA

Trenches
Shoulder-deep trenches stretch over 25 miles (40 km), meandering across the hillside of Den Den. Here a whole town was built underground as the center of the resistance to Ethiopian rule. Five to six fighters lived in underground bunkers not larger than 3.3 by 6.5 feet (1 by 2 m), sleeping, eating, and fighting for 18 months at a time. An incredible memorial to human endurance and courage, Nakfa is rightfully venerated by all Eritreans.

Filfil National Park
Located at an altitude of between 2,296 and 6,562 feet (700 and 2,000 meters), Filfil is the last remnant of Eritrea's tropical rain forest. Here, vervet monkeys and hamadrya baboons are easily seen, as well as gazelles, bushbucks, warthogs, and even leopards. A wide variety of birds make their home in the forest, including most of the Abyssinian endemic species.

Debre Bizen
The Orthodox Monastery of Debre Bizen was founded in 1368. Its library contains more than 1,000 manuscripts as well as various church relics, including crowns, robes, and incense burners. Situated at 7,874 feet (2,400 m) above sea level, the monastery is not open to women or any female creature.

Water Cisterns
One of Eritrea's most ancient relics, the water cisterns number 365, one for every day of the year. Cut from the coral limestone, they catch rainwater and provide the main source of fresh water for the Dahlak islanders. More than 1,000 years old, some are still in use.

Enda Mariam Orthodox Cathedral
Built in 1938, the cathedral displays a blend of Italian and Eritrean architecture. The massive horizontal stone beams are examples of traditional Aksumite architecture as well as traditional stones used as bells. Lovely murals depicting scenes from the Bible adorn the inside walls.

The Stele
Dating from the middle of the first century B.C., the Stele is a structure measuring 15.35 feet (4.68 m) above ground and 3.3 feet (1 m) below. It is unique in Eritrea with its pre-Christian symbol of the sun over a crescent moon. A Geez inscription down the middle dedicates the stele to King Agheze's forefathers. The area around Metera is an important archaeological site, which predates the Aksumite period in some parts. Excavations have unearthed gold objects dating to the second century A.D. as well as Mediterranean amphorae and marble plates.

Lake Badda
Lying below sea level, beautiful Lake Badda was formed in the crater of an extinct volcano, Abuhibet. This turquoise jewel at the edge of the Denakil Depression measures 1,312 feet (400 m) in diameter and, according to an old Italian survey, is 328 feet (100 m) deep. The opposite wall of the crater is solid lava.

ABOUT THE CULTURE

OFFICIAL NAME
State of Eritrea (*Hagere Ertra*)

CAPITAL
Asmara

TOTAL AREA
46,830 square miles (121,320 square km)

POPULATION
5,792,984 (2010 estimate)

ADMINISTRATIVE ZONES
Anseba, Central, Gash-Barka, Northern Red Sea, Southern, and Southern Red Sea

MAJOR CITIES
Asmara, Massawa, Keren, Assab, Agordat, Dekemhare, and Mendefera

MAJOR RIVERS
Anseba, Barka, Gash, and Tekeze

MAJOR LANGUAGES
Afar, Arabic, Tigre and Kunama, Tigrinya, other Cushitic languages

ETHNIC GROUPS
Tigrinya 50 percent, Tigre and Kunama 40 percent, Afar 4 percent, Saho 3 percent, others 3 percent

MAJOR RELIGIONS
Islam 50 percent, Orthodox Christian 40 percent, Roman Catholic 4 percent, Protestant 2 percent, others 4 percent

BIRTH RATE
34.2 births/1,000 population (2010 estimate)

DEATH RATE
8.4 deaths/1,000 population (2010 estimate)

INFANT MORTALITY RATE
Total: 42.3 deaths/1,000 live births
Male: 47.9 deaths/1,000 live births
Female: 36.6 deaths/1,000 live births (2010 estimate)

FERTILITY RATE
4.6 children born/woman (2010 estimate)

LIFE EXPECTANCY
Total population: 62.2 years
Male: 60.1 years
Female: 64.3 years (2010 estimate)

TIME LINE

IN ERITREA	IN THE WORLD
125,000 B.C. Early humans settle near Bay of Zula south of Massawa.	
1000 B.C. Tribes from present-day Yemen migrate to the southern highlands of Eritrea.	
600 B.C. Arabs visit the coast of Eritrea.	
A.D. 300–600 Eritrea is part of the Ethiopian kingdom of Aksum.	
400 Christianity arrives with Syrian merchants.	
600–700 Arabs introduce Islam to coastal areas.	**1206–1368** Genghis Khan unifies the Mongols and starts conquest of the world. At its height, the Mongol Empire under Kublai Khan stretches from China to Persia and parts of Europe and Russia.
1500s Ottoman Empire annexes Eritrea.	
1577 Founding of Sultanate of Awsa, an Afar sultanate, in southeast Eritrea.	**1776** U.S. Declaration of Independence
1869 Italian priest Giuseppe Sapeto buys Assab from local sultan.	
1890 Italian king Umberto declares colony of Eritrea, with Massawa as capital.	**1914** World War I begins.
1935 Mussolini invades Abyssinia from Eritrea, using chemical weapons.	**1939** World War II begins.
1941 British forces defeat Italians at Keren and take over administration of Eritrea.	**1945** The United States drops atomic bombs on Hiroshima and Nagasaki, Japan. World War II ends.
1946 Italy formally renounces all claims to its African colonies.	
1948 Four Powers Commission fails to agree on Eritrea's future.	
1952 Eritrea is federated with Ethiopia under UN-brokered deal.	
1961 Beginning of armed struggle	
1962 Eritrean parliament dissolved. Ethiopia formally annexes Eritrea.	

IN ERITREA	IN THE WORLD
1988	
EPLF smashes Ethiopia's Nadew Command at Afabet, ending military stalemate.	
1991	
EPLF takes Asmara.	
1993	
Formal independence	
1997	**1997**
Eritrea launches it own currency, the Nakfa.	Hong Kong is returned to China.
1998	
Border war with Ethiopia	
2000	
OAU peace treaty signed. UN peacekeepers patrol temporary security zone between Eritrea and Ethiopia.	**2001** Terrorists crash planes into New York; Washington, D.C.; and Pennsylvania.
2003	**2003**
Boundary commission rules that the disputed border town of Badme lies in Eritrea. Ethiopia rejects the ruling.	War in Iraq begins.
2005	
World Food Program warns of a dire food situation after a series of droughts. It extends emergency operations to help more than 840,000 people.	
2007	
Eritrea accepts border line demarcated by international boundary commission; Ethiopia rejects it.	
2008	
UN extends mandate of peacekeepers on Ethiopia-Eritrea border. Fighting breaks out between Djiboutian and Eritrean troops in the disputed Ras Doumeira border area. United States condemns Eritrean "aggression," but Eritrea denies launching an attack.	
2009	
UN Security Council says Eritrea failed to fulfill its obligation to withdraw troops from disputed border area of Djibouti under an ultimatum issued in January. UN imposes sanctions on Eritrea for its alleged support for Islamist insurgents in Somalia and failure to withdraw from Djibouti territory. Eritrea withdraws from Djibouti.	

GLOSSARY

aba'ke (ah-BAH-kay)
An unfermented drink made from a lentil-like grain.

amba (AHM-bah)
A small tableland with steep walls and a flat top.

berbere (bear-BEAR)
A hot sauce made of red chilies.

bun (BOON)
Strong Eritrean coffee.

chira wata (CHEE-ruh WAH-tuh)
A musical instrument similar to the violin.

dadda
A ritual fight between the young men of neighboring villages for a bountiful harvest.

diaspora
The movement or scattering of a group of people from their established homeland.

djellabia (JEL-lah-bay-ah)
A loose, long-sleeved robe for men.

douma (DOE-mah)
A very strong alcohol made by the Afar from the sap of palm trees.

fool (FOOL)
A bean puree.

frittata (FRI-ta-tah)
Scrambled eggs with onions and tomatoes.

injera (in-JEHR-uh)
A bread made from teff, wheat, or sorghum.

kirar (KEE-rahr)
A guitar-like instrument with five strings.

kitcha (KIT-cher)
A very thin unleavened bread baked from wheat or barley.

mido (MEE-doh)
A traditional wooden comb worn by Eritrean men in their hair.

mies (MEES)
An alcoholic beverage made with honey and water.

quno (KOO-noh)
A hairstyle in which the hair is plaited in fine strands close to the scalp and left loose from the nape.

sheleel (SHO-leel)
A group dance in which women shake their long plaited hair vigorously across their faces.

yekeniely (YUH-ke-nee-lih)
An expression of gratitude; literally means "May God keep you."

zigni (ZIHG-nee)
A chicken or beef stew.

FOR FURTHER INFORMATION

BOOKS

Gebremedhin, Tesfa G. *Traditions of Eritrea: Linking the Past to the Future.* Lawrenceville, NJ: Red Sea Press, 2008.

Habte Sillasie, Zeray. *What Is Your Name: Book of Eritrean & Ethiopian Names.* Lawrenceville, NJ: Africa World Press Inc., 2000.

Kibreab, Gaim. *Eritrea: A Dream Deferred.* Oxford: James Currey, 2009.

Pool, Hannah. *My Father's Daughter: A Story of Family and Belonging.* New York: Free Press, 2009.

Schmidt, Peter R., Curtis, Matthew C., and Teka, Zelalem. *The Archaeology of Ancient Eritrea.* Lawrenceville, NJ: Red Sea Press, 2007.

Tesfagiorgis, Mussie G. *Eritrea (Africa in Focus).* Santa Barbara, CA: ABC-CLIO, 2010.

Tesfay, Alemseged. *Two Weeks in the Trenches.* Lawrenceville, NJ: Africa World Press, 2002.

Warren, Olivia. *Taste of Eritrea: Recipes from One of East Africa's Most Interesting Little Countries.* New York: Hippocrene Books, 2000.

White, Ed. *An African Treasure.* New York: Whitehouse Publishing, 2004.

Wrong, Michela. *I Didn't Do It for You.* New York: HarperCollins, 2005.

FILMS

City of Dreams. Directed by Ruby Ofori & Edward Scott. 2006.

Home Across Lands. Directed by John Lavall. 2008.

Mallets in the Mountains — The Eritrean Railway. Produced by Highball Productions. 2010.

MUSIC

Gual Eritrea. Zemichael, Amanuel. Eri Girl. 2005.

BIBLIOGRAPHY

BOOKS

Habte Sillasie, Zeray. *What Is Your Name: Book of Eritrean & Ethiopian Names.* Trenton, New Jersey: Africa World Press Inc., 2000.

Iyob, Ararat. *Blankets of Sand: Poems of War and Exile.* Trenton, New Jersey: Red Sea Press, 1999.

Pateman, Roy. *Eritrea: Even the Stones Are Burning.* Trenton, New Jersey: Red Sea Press, 1998.

Pollera, Alberto. *The Native Peoples of Eritrea* (translated by Linda Lappin). Trenton, New Jersey: Red Sea Press, 2000.

WEBSITES

BBC, http://news.bbc.co.uk/2/hi/africa/country_profiles/1070813.stm

Central Intelligence Agency—Eritrea, www.cia.gov/library/publications/the-world-factbook/geos/er.html

Eritrea Daily, www.eritreadaily.net/

Ethnologue—Languages of Eritrea, www.ethnologue.com/show_country.asp?name=Eritrea

Lonely Planet—Eritrea, www.lonelyplanet.com/eritrea

Shabait: Ministry of Information, www.shabait.com/

U.S. Department of State—Eritrea, http://travel.state.gov/travel/cis_pa_tw/tw/tw_2939.html

University of Pennsylvania—African Studies Center—Eritrea, www.africa.upenn.edu/Country_Specific/Eritrea.html

World Statesmen—Eritrea, www.worldstatesmen.org/Eritrea.html

INDEX

INDEX